Letting Go: Deregulating the Process of Deregulation, or:

Temptation of the Kleptocrats and the Political Economy of Regulatory Disingenuousness

Alfred E. Kahn

1998
MSU Public Utilities Papers

Institute of Public Utilities and Network Industries
The Eli Broad Graduate School of Management
Michigan State University
East Lansing, Michigan

ISBN: 0-87744-182-0

Printed in the United States of America

Contents

Preface

This comprehensive paper has evolved from a keynote presentation delivered by Professor Alfred E. Kahn at the 28th Annual Williamsburg Conference of the Institute of Public Utilities, held on December 4-6, 1996. The original presentation has been expanded and has become, in effect, the third volume of his seminal two-volume series, The Economics of Regulation (New York: John Wiley & Sons, Inc, 1970-71).

In this paper, Professor Kahn offers an analysis of the direction and scope of the changes transforming the telecommunications and electric power industries, together with an evaluation of the regulatory process and policies accompanying these changes. Citing the inconsistencies associated with access charges, price structures, affiliate relationships, and other factors, the author posits that existing regulatory efforts are biased toward demonstrating the immediate benefits of competition at the expense of promoting efficient markets.

The author draws upon the instrumental role that he played in the deregulation movement, most notably in the airline industry, and applies this experience, together with his continuing involvement in reform efforts in telecommunications and electric power, to the task of creating workable markets and institutions that are congruent with economic, technological, social, and political reality.

While others examining the same set of issues might arrive at conclusions different from those set forth by Professor Kahn, this paper constitutes a most important contribution to the debate and to an understanding of public policy as it applies to utilities and network based industries.

Michelle F. Wilsey
Associate Director
Institute of Public Utilities

Letting Go: Deregulating the Process of Deregulation, or:

Temptation of the Kleptocrats and the Political Economy of Regulatory Disingenuousness

Alfred E. Kahn

A few months ago, a movie actor earned an Academy Award by screaming repeatedly into a telephone: "Show me the money!" He has since had a rash of imitators, loudly complaining about the limited results produced so far by the deregulation of the telephone and electric power industries—"Where are the rate reductions?"—protesting that, instead, "telephone deregulation is going to mean higher bills"[1] and that consumers

* Robert Julius Thorne Professor of Political Economy, Emeritus, Cornell University; Special Consultant, National Economic Research Associates, Inc. (NERA). Formerly member of the national Economic Advisory Council to AT&T (1968-74), Chairman of the New York Public Service Commission, 1974-77 and from 1981 onward, consultant to and witness in various regulatory proceedings for the Regional Bell Operating Companies (RBOCs). Preparation of this paper has been supported in part by the Edison Electric Institute and the Institute of Public Utilities. I thank Jonathan Falk, Dennis L. Weisman, Willie Grieve, Robert W. Crandall, Paul Vasington, Timothy J. Tardiff, Augustin Ros and Neil Zoltowski for their invaluable assistance, comments and, in some instances, active collaboration, and must single out Joel Brainard for especial thanks for his extraordinarily detailed, challenging and insightful criticisms.

I have come to think of this paper, reflecting some 20 to 25 years of active experience with economic regulation and deregulation, as constituting, in effect, a sequel and third volume of my *The Economics of Regulation*, originally published in 1970-71. At the same time, I feel compelled to acknowledge that its discussions of the highly contentious issues associated with the deregulation of telecommunications and electric power will, despite a conscientious effort to maintain academic impartiality, inevitably reflect my long association during the intervening years as consultant with incumbent utility companies.

[1] Mark Landler, *The New York Times*, March 30, 1997, p. A1.

would end up "shafted."[2] Not to be outdone, the Heritage Foundation in January 1997 cited estimates that consumers ought by then to have been enjoying reductions in electric rates greater than 25 percent in the short-run—and weren't.[3]

Apart from the justifiable skepticism that these various predictions and complaints reflect about the willingness of public utility companies to cooperate in surrendering their legally conferred monopolies, they exhibit a deplorable failure to understand—or, if they understand, fully to reveal—where those hoped-for benefits to consumers would have had to come from and how competition confers its real benefits on the public at large, as distinguished from benefiting some at the expense of others.

The impatience that these complaints reflect and feed generate powerful temptations of politically motivated regulators to produce quick and large "consumer benefits" by, in effect, expropriating stockholders' assets—a phenomenon that might be characterized as a temptation of the kleptocrats.

As I demonstrated by the role I played in the deregulation of the airline and trucking industries, I yield to no one in the intensity of my conviction that competition is a better safeguard and promoter of the interest of both consumers and the public at large than regulated monopoly, wherever it is feasible—that is, except in cases where monopoly is natural, because competitive duplication of facilities would be grossly inefficient. Indeed, newly liberated competition can, in some circumstances, produce large and quick net public benefits. In the decade before they were deregulated, for example, the airlines had greatly increased their capacity by substituting jets and jumbo jets for their prop equipment. That, along with the slowdown in the growth of demand in the mid-1970s, left them with large numbers of empty seats. In the 13 years before deregulation, the U.S. trunk carriers filled an average of only 53.3

---

[2] The actual prediction, by the chairman of a state utility commission, was: "The game is called 'shift and shaft'.... You shift the costs to the states and shaft the consumer." *Ibid.*, p. A15.

[3] Adam D. Thierer, "Energizing America: A Blueprint for Deregulating the Electricity Market," The Heritage Foundation, *Backgrounder* No. 1100, Jan. 23, 1997, p. 4.

percent of their seats with fare-paying passengers.[4] Once deregulation gave them freedom—and subjected them to competitive pressure—to do so, they engaged in an orgy of discounting, which has become ever more nearly universal: last year, 94 percent of all mileage flown was at discount fares, averaging only 30 percent of the full coach levels; load factors had climbed to 69.8 percent[5] and, Clifford Winston and Steven Morrison estimate, travelers have in the aggregate benefited, on balance, to the tune of some \$12.4 billion (1993) a year.[6]

This is of course not the whole airline story. The major qualifications are that the full fares, from which the average discount is calculated, have risen much farther than would be likely to have been permitted had regulation continued, and planes have become more congested and flying less comfortable (but the schedules not less convenient). But those discomforts were a necessary part of the bargain we sought to achieve—the provision of ubiquitous lower-quality/lower-price options, thitherto suppressed by regulation—the response to which by the overwhelming majority of travelers has carried the day. Meanwhile, competition has, over time, forced the carriers to restore the high-price/high-quality option as well—with frequent traveler awards; separate, shorter lines at the ticket counter; and automatic upgrades to first class.

The same thing happened when regulators, beginning in New York, California and at the federal level, made the local telephone companies permit customers to attach their own phones, answering machines and computers to the telephone network. It is difficult for most of us to remember when the only choice was to lease these from AT&T at rates far in excess of costs—when, if, and as it chose to make them available at all.

Competition can produce immediate benefits also when the previous regulatory regimes either tolerated or imposed gross inefficiencies or

---

[4] Calculated from Air Transport Association, *Annual Reports, Air Transport*.

[5] *Ibid.* and data for Nov. 1996 through Oct. 1997 from Air Transport Association, *Monthly Discount and Yield Report*, Oct. 1997.

[6] Steven A. Morrison and Clifford Winston, *The Evolution of the Airline Industry*, Washington: Brookings, 1995, p. 13.

permitted monopolistic profits. Removal of the minutely detailed restrictions on the routes that each regulated airline and trucker was permitted to traverse and on the cargo each was permitted to carry, along with the intensified pressures of price competition that deregulation unleashed, led to massive realignments of route structures, the ability to offer service between a greater number of origins and destinations and fuller use of capacity—the latter encouraged also by the freedom it gave carriers to offer lower rates for seats or trucking space that would otherwise go unutilized. Intensified competition has also exerted powerful downward pressure on inflated wages, as well as for the elimination of cost-inflating work practices and, in the case of truckers, high profits, all of which were previously insulated by restrictions on competitive pricing and entry.[7]

---

[7] See Morrison and Winston, *op. cit.*; Winston, Corsi, Grimm and Evans, *The Economic Effects of Surface Freight Deregulation*, Washington: Brookings, 1990; Winston, "Economic Deregulation: Day of Reckoning for Microeconomists," *Journal of Economic Literature*, Vol. 31 (Sept. 1993), pp. 1263-89; Robert W. Crandall and Jerry Ellig, *Economic Deregulation and Customer Choice: Lessons for the Electric Industry*, Center for Market Processes, George Mason University, 1997; and Kahn, "Deregulation: Looking Backward and Looking Forward," *Yale Journal on Regulation*, Vol. 7 (1990), pp. 325-54.

I. Where the Money is: the Temptation of the Kleptocrats

Competition may confidently be expected to subject the electric and telephone companies as well to greater pressure to improve their efficiency than they were subject to under traditional cost-plus, rate-of-return regulation. The combination of free entry and the abandonment of cost-plus is likely to be far more conducive also to innovation, particularly in the exploitation of the dynamic telecommunications technology. But competition produces benefits such as these only gradually and over time[8]; these are not the possibilities of immediate, large rate reductions whose failure to appear quickly in these industries has generated such disappointment and political pressure for quick results. That is not where the money is.

The big money—hundreds of billions of dollars in total, translating into scores of billions of dollars a year annually—is the capitalized sunk

---

[8] For a judgment that "restructuring for competition and regulatory reform is unlikely to lead to significant short-run cost savings," and that "the opportunities for costs [*sic*] savings in the United States in the medium run are significant, but not enormous"—but that "the most important opportunities for cost savings are associated with long-run investments in generating capacity," related in important measure to abandoning the traditional regulatory arrangements that "implicitly allocate ... most of the market risks associated with investments in generating capacity to consumers rather than producers," see Paul L. Joskow, "Restructuring, Competition and Regulatory Reform in the U.S. Electricity Sector," *Journal of Economic Perspectives*, Vol. 11, No. 3 (Summer 1997), pp. 124-25.

For a less cautious assessment of the short-run efficiency gains achieved and achievable in deregulated industries that nevertheless demonstrates also that they tend to become much larger over time, see Clifford Winston, "U.S. Industry Adjustment to Economic Deregulation," *Journal of Economic Perspectives*, Vol. 12, No. 2 (Spring 1998), forthcoming. For an even more sharply contrasting contention or at least implication that despite passage of the Public Utility Regulatory Policies Act of 1978 (see pp. 18-19, below), there remain major opportunities for efficient cogeneration making use of by-product heat now largely wasted, the exploitation of which awaits removal of the present obstacles to competition, see Thomas R. Casten and Mark C. Hall, "Barriers to Deploying More Efficient Electrical Generation and Combined Heat and Power Plants," Trigen Energy Corp., White Plains, NY (undated).

costs incurred over past decades by the electric and telephone utilities in excess of what the current market value of those assets would be under open competition.

In the case of the electric companies these are, preponderantly, costs of what have turned out to be mistakes, because of:

1. the entry into service of long-lead-time base-load generating plants, constructed over a period of double-digit inflation of interest rates and construction costs and in anticipation of a continued expansion of demand at 6 percent to 7 percent annual rates that never materialized. These developments and the abrupt deceleration of demand left utilities, particularly on the East and West coasts, with average generating costs in the range of 6 to 10 cents a kWh and, because of their excess capacity, short-run marginal costs of 1 to 2 cents;

2. the collapse of fossil fuel prices in the middle 1980s, in combination with

3. the development of combined cycle gas turbine technology, which has made it possible to build 100-megawatt or smaller new plants with average costs below 4 cents a kWh;

4. the wide gap between expectations and results of nuclear plants and

5. the Public Utility Regulatory Policies Act of 1978 (PURPA), with its legacy of multibillion-dollar contractual obligations of the electric companies to buy more independently generated power than it turns out they need, at avoided costs estimated by regulators on the basis (among other considerations) of an expectation that the price of oil would by now be approaching $100 a barrel.[9]

---

[9] In the interest of completeness, I should mention the often very large volume of "regulatory assets" on the books of the utility companies—expenses (such as for fuel, taxes and post-retirement employee benefits) capitalized for rate-making purposes rather than contemporaneously recovered from ratepayers. These are, in effect, regulatory promises to pay the utility companies in the form of a return on and of those deferrals over time.

All these developments have combined to produce regulated rates, in some regions of the country, far above the levels that would prevail under free competition—the short- and long-run marginal costs of the incumbent companies themselves as well as of their challengers. That has created irresistible temptations for sellers—including utility companies *outside* their own franchise territories—to offer eager buyers an escape from those inflated rates and for buyers to take advantage of the opportunities to shop around for these bargains. Those possibilities have, in turn, subjected regulators and legislatures to corresponding pressures to permit them to do so, leaving the associated sunk costs of the utility companies "stranded," to be absorbed by their stockholders.[10]

The telephone companies, similarly, have on their books the huge capitalized costs of their universally ubiquitous networks, on which they are supposed to have been afforded a reasonable opportunity to earn a return,[11] depreciated historically at rates grossly inadequate for industries

---

[10] See William J. Baumol, Paul L. Joskow and Alfred E. Kahn. "The Challenge for Federal and State Regulators: Transition from Regulation to Efficient Competition in Electric Power," Edison Electric Institute, Dec. 9, 1994. Thierer is quite explicit about this being the preponderant source of the huge potential benefits to consumers that he identifies as immediately available. *Op. cit.*, p. 26. Michael T. Maloney and Robert E. McCormick, upon whose estimates he relies, cite likely short-term benefits to consumers under two different scenarios at $22 and $58 billion annually—of which all but $1.9 and $7.5 billion, respectively, would come out of the pockets of producers in the form of losses of stranded costs (and the costs of producing the additional power consumers would demand at the reduced prices). With Raymond D. Saver, *Customer Choice, Consumer Value: An Analysis of Retail Competition in America's Electric Industry*, Washington: Citizens for a Sound Economy, undated, Volume I, p. xxiii. In contrast, of the $20 billion (1988 dollars) estimated benefits to shippers and final consumers from the deregulation of surface transportation, only some $4 billion, net, was at the expense of reduced profits and the railroad and motor carrier labor forces. Winston, Corsi, Grimm and Evans, *op. cit.*, p. 41. The by no means negligible estimated net benefits to consumers in the electric case reflect the improvement in allocative efficiency produced by the projected rate reductions: economic efficiency is not a zero-sum gain. See also note 22, below.

[11] See the references in note 16, below, to the current heated controversies about this asserted entitlement, both historically and under present circumstances. Subject to the qualification that it was never absolute, I am unaware of any serious contention that the general understanding was other than as I have described it.

operating under such a dynamic technology.[12] As in the case of electric power, the result—that the net or depreciated *book* value of these assets is far greater than what their market value would be in a competitive regime—created no problems so long as the industry was a monopoly. But the more pervasive the entry by competitors carrying no such burden of costs inherited from the past, the greater the difficulty of the incumbent companies recovering those costs except as regulators have taken pains to impose the same burdens on their challengers.

The big money in the telephone industry is to be found also in the structure of rates designed explicitly by regulators to subsidize basic residential service with monopoly markups on other services—particularly long-distance and charges to business customers, especially in concentrated metropolitan areas, where the density of both subscribers and traffic tend to make the average cost of providing a dial tone relatively low. I will allude later to the continuing controversies—marked by a deplorable amount of casuistry, insofar as the contentions are purportedly grounded in economics—about whether the former rates are indeed subsidized. But the market has itself provided the definitive resolution: it has not been an accident that when telephone markets were opened, it was to the latter markets that competitors flocked.

After AT&T was broken up, both the FCC and the state commissions ensured the continuing flow of subsidy by authorizing the local companies to incorporate a similarly inflated markup in their charges to the long-distance companies for access to their networks for the origination and termination of calls. Unsurprisingly, therefore, the long-distance companies, on the one side, and big business customers, on the other, began bypassing the facilities of the telephone companies and interconnecting directly with one another in order to evade those inflated charges. Today, every major metropolitan area in the country has its own competitive provider of access for long-distance calls, and these so-called CAPs are now also offering basic local dial tone service to business customers.

---

[12] *The NTIA Infrastructure Report: Telecommunications in The Age of Information,,* National Telecommunications and Information Administration, Publication 91-26 (Oct. 1991), pp. 254-59.

It was precisely in recognition of the likelihood that much of this bypass was or would be uneconomic—induced not by the comparative *costs* of the telephone companies and their competitors but by the inflated *rates* of the former—that the FCC in the '80s imposed the $3.50 a month "subscriber line charge" that still appears on all our residential bills, explicitly in order to be able to reduce the interstate access charges correspondingly.[13]

The welfare consequences of this distorted pricing structure are huge. The estimates of the direct welfare losses caused by the overpricing of relatively demand-elastic services run in the range of $8 to $10 billion annually. Crandall and Waverman put the total annual drain on the economy—taking into account indirect, dynamic consequences—at $30 billion.[14]

Whatever the possible justification for the below-cost pricing of basic residential services historically, when only a minority of households had telephones, it serves no such purpose today when subscribership is well above 90 percent. The demand for telephone service is highly inelastic, and recent studies have suggested it is probably at least as sensitive to the level of long-distance charges as of the basic monthly charge.[15] The majority of subscriber cut-offs, for example, has been occasioned by their failure to pay long-distance bills.

---

[13] *In the Matter of MTS and WATS Market Structure, Amendment to Part 67 of the Commission's Rules and Establishment of a Joint Board,* CC Docket No. 78-72, 80-286, 2 FCC Rcd 2953, adopted April 16, 1987, corrected June 10, 1987.

[14] Robert W. Crandall and Leonard Waverman, *Talk Is Cheap,* Washington: Brookings, 1996. The full meaning of the title of their book is "Talk *Ought to be* Cheap but Isn't Because of our Perverse Regulatory Policies."

[15] For example, Hausman, Tardiff and Belinfante found that the rate rebalancing associated with the FCC's subscriber line charge program, which produced large reductions in long-distance prices associated with a corresponding increase in basic service charges, had the effect of *increasing* telephone subscribership. "The Effects of the Breakup of AT&T on Telephone Penetration in the United States," *American Economic Review,* Vol. 83 (May 1993), pp. 178-184. This conclusion has been corroborated by R.E. Eriksson, D.L. Kaserman, and J.W. Mayo, "Targeted and Untargeted Subsidy Schemes: Evidence from Post-Divestiture Efforts to Promote Universal Telephone Service," Department of Economics, University of Tennessee, October 1995, who found that untargeted subsidies—aimed at holding down basic rates generally, as contrasted with targeted (i.e., needs tested) subsidies—financed at the expense of long-distance usage had the net effect of reducing subscribership.

The intensely contested issue of whether the incumbent utility companies—both electric and telephone—are or are not, or should or should not, to be entitled to recovery of those sunk costs has been and continues to be thoroughly explored in the literature and testimony before regulatory agencies. I make no effort to retrace those arguments here.[16] It suffices for

---

[16] See, for example, Baumol, Joskow and Kahn, *op. cit.*; and the exchanges on the pages of *Regulation*, 1996, Nos. 1-4 and my "Competition and Stranded Costs Revisited," *Natural Resource Journal*, 1997 forthcoming. In the telephone case, the controversies center on whether the charges by the local exchange companies for access to their networks or for leases of unbundled elements of their networks to would-be competitors should incorporate markups above incremental costs to contribute to the recovery of sunk costs and to compensate for the underpricing of basic residential service. See, on the one side, David Gabel, *Competition-Enhancing Costing and Pricing Standards for Telecommunications Interconnection*, National Regulatory Research Institute, NRRI, 96-22, September 1996, pp. 13-17, and the criticisms of that position by Aniruddha Banerjee, "Costing and Pricing Principles for Competitive Telecommunications: A Critique of David Gabel's Recommendations," National Economic Research Associates, Inc., March 1, 1997, pp. 24-29. By my standards (see note 17, below), Gabel's is an invitation to kleptocratic behavior. One aspect of this highly contentious issue that is likely to become increasingly prominent as Congress moves to legislate deregulation of the electric industry is the proper balance between the roles of the federal and state governments, particularly in resolving stranded cost issues. In general, defenders of the right of the utility companies to such recoveries tend to argue that the proper locus for resolution of the issue and provision for recovery is at the state level, on the grounds—which seem to me unexceptionable—that (1) it is the several state commissions that have had and continue to have the responsibility for determining those entitlements and (2) it is possible to provide for recovery of such costs in ways that would be competitively neutral—that is to say, that would not conflict with a national policy of deregulation. While, as this last observation demonstrates, advocates of deregulated competition can come down on either side of the jurisdictional issue, those who tend to be hostile to stranded cost recovery argue for some degree of federal preemption of these issues, in order to prevent individual states from preserving their regimes of franchised monopoly as a means of enabling the utility companies to recover their historically incurred costs.

The identical jurisdictional issue was bitterly contested during the course of 1997 as it applied to telecommunications deregulation. The Telecommunications Reform Act of 1996 prescribed private negotiations, arbitration and approval by the State utility commissions of the terms on which the incumbent local telephone companies (ILECs) were to give competitors access to their networks in the several ways it stipulated. (See Section II.C., below.) The FCC attempted to prescribe the method by which those rates were to be set and actually established proxy rates that were to be adopted by the states if they did not use its prescribed method; neither of these made explicit provision for the recovery of costs—both sunk and ongoing—actually incurred by the

(continued...)

my purposes to point out that this is where the big money—the possibility of large, quick rate reductions—is. The result is my version of *The Bonfire*

(*...continued*)

companies. Several state commissions successfully sought a stay by the Circuit Court of Appeals of the FCC's Order on both jurisdictional and substantive grounds. *Iowa Utilities Board et al. v. FCC et al.*, U.S. Court of Appeals, Eight Circuit, July 17 and Oct. 14, 1997. I discuss the substantive issues at length in Section III.C., below.

As an advocate of competition, I tend to favor the exercise of federal authority to ensure its uniform adoption nationally. It is impossible to conceive how deregulation of the airlines could have been as efficacious as it proved to be had the individual states been permitted to protect airlines within their jurisdiction from competition. Some protagonists of federal preemption argue, however, as though the mere provision for recovery of "stranded costs"—strictly, costs that would be left stranded by unrestricted competition, in the absence of special provision for their recovery—by imposition of markups in charges for access to such bottleneck facilities as electric transmission and distribution lines would be in itself inconsistent with transformation of the industry to a competitive regime:

> Although states clearly have the right to *study* the future health of in-state utilities, they do not have the right to impose discriminatory taxes on out-of-state consumers or competitors in order to bail out in-state utilities.

> Yet this is exactly what many states across the country are thinking of doing ....

> [The] important question ... is whether the manner in which states are proposing to pay for this corporate welfare poses a potentially unconstitutional threat to interstate commerce. This is because many states are considering paying for stranded cost losses through cost recovery mechanisms that could impose discriminatory taxes on out-of-state carriers ....For example, a number of states are considering higher fees and taxes on transmission line transactions that often are interstate in nature .... Producers operating outside California, for example, could be forced to pay discriminatory transmission charges on power they wheel into the state to help bail out their potential competitors. The market price of power would be raised artificially, and new entry into the market would be discouraged ....

Adam D. Thierer, "Electricity Deregulation and Federalism: How Congress and the States can work together to Deregulate Successfully," Heritage Foundation *Backgrounder* No. 1125, June 23, 1997, pp. 19-20 (stress supplied).

Entirely apart from its grudging concession to the states of the right only to "study the future health of in-state utilities," rather than provide for their continuing recovery of costs that they have heretofore been entitled by long-standing regulatory policy to recover, this argument simply ignores the demonstration in the extensive literature on efficient component pricing that the imposition on competitors—instate or out of state—of charges for access to bottleneck facilities *no larger* than the corresponding markups above incremental costs incorporated in the regulatorily approved rates of the incumbent companies is not a barrier to competition by equally efficient rivals. On the contrary, it is *necessary* in order to prevent *less efficient* rivals taking customers

(*continued...*)

of The Vanities—the Temptation of the Kleptocrats[17]—a temptation to which some regulators have been resistant and others more prone to capitulate.

Entirely apart from this dominating question, these developments raise a serious economic question: How can one know whether the resulting competition is on the basis of the true relative efficiency of the several contestants? The sunk costs and the costs of providing basic residential telephone service at non-compensatory rates, which inflate the other rates of the incumbent companies, have nothing to do with whether social efficiency is improved by their losing customers to competitors unencumbered by that legacy or those obligations. Competitors are flocking into telecommunications and electric markets whose rates have, because of regulatory policies, far exceeded the marginal costs of the incumbent utility companies themselves. In both these industries, inefficient entry could readily be forestalled if the incumbents were to price the cross-subsidizing or sunk cost-recovering services down to their own marginal costs, as regulators are increasingly—and in varying degrees—permitting them to do. The problem, of course, is that by so doing they would be surrendering recovery of billions of dollars of costs that they believe they are entitled—and under obligation to their stockholders to try—to collect.[18]

(*...continued*)

away from incumbents because the rates they can charge are not burdened, as are those of the incumbents, by the latter's regulatory entitlement—and responsibility to their stockholders—to attempt to recover their regulatorily legitimized, non-incremental costs. On the need and the efficacy of the Efficient Component Pricing Rule as a guarantor of competitive parity, see Baumol, Joskow and Kahn, *op. cit.*, pp. 49-54 and the fuller discussion in Sections II.D. and IV.B., below.

[17] As this characterization clearly conveys—despite my declaration of intention not to re-enter here the controversies over the entitlement of utility companies to a reasonable opportunity to recover their costs except as commissions find them imprudent—I regard it as simply undeniable that a general understanding to that effect has been inherent in historical regulatory practice, although by no means absolutely and invariably (see, e.g., my "Who Should Pay for Power-Plant Duds?," *The Wall Street Journal*, Aug. 15, 1985, Op-Ed section, and the sources cited in note 16, above). The "Traditional Issues in the Pricing of Public Utility Services," which are the subject of the second chapter of my *The Economics of Regulation* (John Wiley, 1970, reprinted by the MIT Press, 1988, Vol. I), are, precisely, issues in the interpretation and measurement of the costs recoverable in commission-set rates.

[18] On the difference, in this regard, between the portions of these costs that are, respectively, sunk and ongoing, see note 158 below.

In these circumstances, there is a special irony in the loud complaints by such organizations as the Consumer Federation of America at the slow progress of competition in the local telephone markets since passage of the Telecommunications Act[19] and at the paucity of results in the form of reductions in basic monthly charges for residential service. In the absence of alternative schemes for financing provision of that subsidized service—such as the Act calls for in its "universal service" provisions (see Part V., below)—one would hardly expect competitors to flock into offering a service currently subsidized to the tune of more than $20 billion a year by overcharging others.[20] Of course, to the extent that the inadequacy of the

---

[19] Mark Landler, "Monopolies Still Rule the Local Phone Markets," *New York Times*, May 22, 1997, p. D1.

[20] I make no effort to adequately summarize the many estimates of the size of this subsidy, in part because it would require distinguishing

(1) what would constitute a subsidy in strict economic terms—the extent to which rates fall short of incremental costs—from

(2) the larger amount by which revenues from basic residential service generally, and basic service to residences and businesses in rural areas particularly, fall short of second-best efficient levels—which (as a general proposition) call for markups above incremental costs for the several services inversely proportional to their demand elasticities, to the extent required to recover total costs—from, again,

(3) the amount by which revenues from these services fall short of fully distributed costs—which differ from the others, among other reasons, because of their incorporation of many billion dollars a year of return on and of sunk costs.

One such estimate, prepared by Robert Blau of Bell South from materials assembled by the U.S. Telephone Association, calculates a contribution (above fully distributed costs) from carrier access charges at the federal level of $5 billion in a "recent year" (evidently something like a composite of 1995 and 1996), $8 billion from intrastate toll and carrier access charges, and $9 billion from "vertical and other services"—a total of $22 billion—toward the cost of providing basic services to residences *and* businesses together.

Since (a) the fully distributed costs of these contribution-contributing services almost certainly contain markups above their incremental costs greater than would be called for by second-best efficiency (Ramsey) rules (because of their relatively elastic demand) and (b) the subsidized "basic services" lumped together in this estimate are for households and businesses (the latter of which probably make a contribution to the former) it seems that the $22 billion figure grossly understates the extent to which the former services are overpriced and basic residential service underpriced, relative to what economic efficiency would dictate.

(continued...)

basic monthly charge is offset by the entrée that it gives a telephone company to sales of the overpriced services used by these same customers, as it may be for the majority of them, that impediment is removed; but not if it is possible for competitors to gain that same entrée costlessly, by using the facilities or reselling the offerings of the incumbent, at favorable wholesale rates (see III.C. and IV.C., below). In any event, the net subsidy flow is from business to residential subscribers in the aggregate, and to rural residential customers most egregiously. In these circumstances, the expressions of disappointment by the CFA at the failure of anything remotely approximating genuine, ubiquitous competition for residential customers to appear are worse than unrealistic; they are schizophrenic.

The only opportunities for comparatively quick and large *social welfare* gains in telecommunications, as contrasted with merely transferring dollars from stockholders to ratepayers by reneging on their historical obligation to give the incumbent local exchange companies (ILECs) a fair opportunity to recover their costs, would be if regulators were to risk what some of them obviously fear would be a political firestorm[21] by rebalancing their present inefficient rate structures. It doesn't take much imagination to see the real danger that, under heavy political pressure to show quick results, they will, opportunistically, choose the first course—

(*...continued*)

This last supposition is apparently confirmed by a more recent estimate that the contribution from intraLATA toll and inter- and intrastate switched access services alone, measured by the difference between revenues and their *incremental* costs, amounted to $23.6 billion in 1995. (John Haring and Jeffrey H. Rohlfs, "Economic Perspectives on Access Charge Reform," prepared for BellSouth Telecommunications, Strategic Policy Research, Jan. 29, 1997, p. 13.) The difference between this figure and the $13 billion estimated by Blau would logically be explicable by his using fully distributed costs as the base.

On the other hand, various litigants, and MCI in particular, contend that $20 billion would be a gross exaggeration, (a) typically on the basis of models purporting to measure the cost of completely replicating telephone networks using today's technology, and therefore ignoring the LECs' enormous sunk costs; and (b) evidently also by crediting basic service with net revenues from overpriced complementary services, as MCI witnesses have advocated in other proceedings (See Part III.A.3 and IV.C, below.) See the discussion of their proffered measure of cost in Part III.C., below.

[21] On whether the fear is justified, see Part V.B., below

for example, cut the prices they have heretofore permitted the ILECs to charge competitors for access to their facilities—without biting the bullet of raising the basic residential rates that those concededly inefficiently high charges have subsidized heretofore.[22]

---

[22] This characterization of the two alternatives overstates the contrast between them in one important respect. Letting competition strand the heavy sunk costs of the incumbent utility companies and drive down the prices of the cross-subsidizing services would in itself enormously increase allocative efficiency, on balance, by removing the present inefficient discouragement of consumption by prices far in excess of marginal cost. Against that benefit would have to be weighed the essentially imponderable discouragement of future investments by the government's having, in effect, opportunistically changed the rules of the regulatory game in this way.

II. Micromanaging the Entry and Survival of Competitors

Second only to the temptations of regulators to show results in the form of quick rate reductions—and sometimes actually conflicting with it—is the temptation to produce some competitors, even competitors less efficient than the incumbents, by extending to them special preferences or protections and restraining efficient competitive responses by the incumbents.

This was a temptation we were able to avoid entirely, in the case of transportation, because we eventually conceived (more accurately, we were forced by the inexorably cumulative process of deregulation, once initiated, to conceive) that we could essentially dismantle the entire superstructure of controls—licensure of entry, restrictive stipulation of operating rights, prescription of prices and conditions of service—without residual need for direct regulatory protections of either customers or competitors.[23] The absence of any significant political move to reverse those steps strongly suggests that we were essentially right. I have elsewhere recounted how we came to that realization in the case of the airlines, beginning with the intention of moving gradually and deliberately; discovering that doing so created more problems than it solved; and how the process, once initiated, took on a life of its own, until there appeared to be no halfway house between comprehensive regulation on the one side and something close to total deregulation on the other.[24]

---

[23] The one significant exception was the clause in the Staggers Act directing the Interstate Commerce Commission to set ceilings on the railroad rates charged captive shippers. See James N. Heller, *Coal Transportation and Deregulation: An Impact of the Staggers Act*, Washington, D.C.: The Energy Bureau and Sherif Press, 1983, Chapter 4.

[24] See, e.g., my "Applications of Economics to an Imperfect World," (The Richard T. Ely lecture, *The American Economic Review, Papers and Proceedings*, Vol. 69, No. 2, May 1979, pp. 1-13); and the "The Uneasy Marriage of Regulation and Competition," *Telematics*, Washington, D.C., September 1984, pp. 1-2, 8-17.

(*continued...*)

It is clearly not possible to totally eliminate direct regulation of what we have traditionally considered to be the authentic public utilities. The reason, of course, has been the persistence of monopoly, particularly in the local distribution networks and also in electric transmission, which has required continuing regulation for two closely related reasons:

- to protect captive, principally residential and small business, customers;

- to ensure fair and efficient competition between the integrated utility companies and challengers dependent upon access to their monopolized or partially-monopolized facilities, including safeguarding against cross-subsidization of that competition by the incumbent utilities at the expense of their monopoly customers.

The conceded need for these continued restraints and obligations on the incumbent public utility companies, in the interest of ensuring equally efficient rivals a fair opportunity to compete, in effect imposes on regulators a positive *responsibility* for the introduction of competition that goes far beyond simply getting out of the way, as was critical contribution in the transportation industries. In these circumstances, they have, with

---

(...continued)
In the case of trucking, it was some 14 years before direct regulation within recalcitrant individual states was finally eliminated, along with the formal requirement that all tariffs be publicly filed at the Interstate Commerce Commission. This latter requirement was widely ignored, once carriers were freed to set their own rates and to negotiate long-term contracts with individual shippers. Its retention—including the technical legal obligation of truckers to adhere to those filed tariffs—had the embarrassing consequence, as large numbers of truckers went into receivership under pressure of competition, of lawyers acting on behalf of their creditors seeking out the favored shippers and presenting them with bills for illegally received rebates totaling some $32 billion dollars, according to the estimates of the ICC. It took an additional intervention by Congress, in the form of the Negotiated Rates Act, to exempt shippers from these obligations unless and until the ICC found the officially filed rates reasonable, thereby bringing to a close what threatened to be an extremely expensive lesson in the dangers of only partial economic deregulation. Daniel Pearl, "Congress Conferees Agree on Ending State and Local Trucking Regulation," *Wall Street Journal*, Aug. 5, 1994, p. B4; James Bovard, "The Great Truck Robbery," *Wall Street Journal*, Nov. 3, 1993, p. A22; and "White House Clears Negotiated Rates Act, Covering Truck Fees," *Wall Street Journal*, Dec. 6, 1993, p. B7.

worrisome consistency, erred on the side of protecting or giving a special boost to *competitors* that might not otherwise survive unbiased competition of the incumbents—a bias facilitated by the inherent difficulty of distinguishing the protecting of competitors from efficient and from unfair competition.[25]

A particularly poignant example of both the need for and the pitfalls of regulatory intervention in such circumstances is provided by the experience under the provisions of the Public Utility Regulatory Policies Act of 1978 requiring incumbent electric power companies to purchase independently produced power from qualifying generating facilities at prices based on the generating costs they would avoid by so doing.

The need for the requirement, under the prevailing system of rate base/rate of return regulation of the utility companies, was clear. Since company profits were a direct function of the size of their rate bases, the system encouraged them to build big, capital-intensive plants[26]—even to the point of their feeling compelled to complete nuclear plants that might better have been abandoned, under the threat that they would otherwise be excluded from rate base because they were not "used and useful." They also had no incentive in that situation to seek out and buy cheaper power, even at prices lower than their own avoidable costs, because those cost savings would have merely flowed through to their customers and the reduction in their own production would have jeopardized the return on their investments. *Given* the irrationality of that system, PURPA made sense. It took governmental compulsion to make the companies purchase independently generated power whenever it made economic sense for them to do so; this also required regulatory agencies to set the prices of those purchases.

The necessary intervention, however, lead to multi-billion dollar errors, in part because of a deliberate policy of giving a special boost to the entry of independent generators and in part inadvertently—to what extent it was

---

[25] Joel B. Dirlam and A.E. Kahn, *Fair Competition, the Law and Economics of Antitrust Policy*, Ithaca: Cornell University Press, 1954.

[26] See the discussion of the so-called Averch-Johnson effect in my *The Economics of Regulation*, Vol. II, pp. 49-59.

the one motive or cause and to what extent the other, I am unable to say. New York State, for example, stipulated a price of six cents a kilowatt hour at which the incumbent utility companies were required to purchase independently generated power. In consideration of the special problems of entrants and, in particular, the need to raise capital on favorable terms, many states required the incumbent utility companies to enter into long-term contracts, with stipulated indexation clauses, enabling the entrants to finance themselves almost entirely with debt, and erred consciously on the side of generosity in their estimates of the avoidable costs or the prescribed floor for those purchase prices.[27] In addition, confronted with the policy decision to stipulate the contractual terms for years into the future rather than letting the transactions be consummated at marginal costs determined on a real time basis, they made genuine errors in projecting those avoided costs. These turned out mostly on the side of generosity—unsurprisingly, in consideration of the perceived energy crisis during the course of which PURPA was passed and the widespread expectations that the price of oil might by the end of the century reach $100 a barrel.[28]

So, as characteristically happens, a regulatory system with severe imperfections elicited a plausible remedy that has turned out worse than the disease it was intended to cure.[29] Clearly, the more rational solution would have been to correct the distortion of utility company incentives inherent in rate base/rate of return regulation: a system of rate caps, for example, would have eliminated the preference for "making" rather than "buying."

---

[27] See the account of the similarly perverse application of the same avoided cost statutory standard by the Federal Communications Commission in Section III.C.2., below.

[28] See Paul L. Joskow, "Regulatory Failure, Regulatory Reform, and Structural Change in the Electrical Power Industry" in *Brookings Papers on Economic Activity*, Martin Neil Baily and Clifford Winston, Editors, Washington, DC: Brookings Institution, 1989, pp. 163-174. In these circumstances, it would be unconscionable to force the shareholders of the utility companies to absorb the costs of those regulatory errors, even under the "guilty if not 100 percent innocent" rule recommended by opponents of stranded cost recovery for application to nuclear plants: that any utility claiming a nuclear stranding be required to show that regulators gave it no choice but to build or complete the plant despite the utility's preference for an alternative (Robert Michaels, "Stranded Investments, Stranded Intellectuals," *Regulation*, 1996 No. 1, p. 49).

[29] On the other hand, by clearly demonstrating the economic feasibility of independent
(*continued...*)

A. "Infant Company" Protection

The tendency of regulators to err on the side of giving special preferences or protections to entrants has no doubt been influenced also by the valid theoretical case that can be made in favor of providing temporary preferences usually characterized as the infant industry exception to the rule on unbiased competition. This refers to the possibility that an inexperienced, fledgling industry may require temporary insulation from competition or some handicapping of the competitive struggle to its advantage, if it is to have a fair opportunity to acquire sufficient experience and market position to enable it, ultimately, to survive without that protection.

Proposals such as these and their proposed application to fledgling companies are not refutable in principle. It is not possible to state that the "infant company" hypothesis is simply incorrect. The decision of whether new competitors should be given that sort of preference in any specific case is an empirical one; it necessarily involves an exercise of judgment in the light of the specific circumstances of each case—a judgment of the extent to which the promised future benefits of the competition ensured by this kind of temporary protection of competitors (properly discounted for the fact that they will accrue only in the future and are subject to inevitable uncertainty) outweigh the immediate cost to consumers of handicapping the incumbent, challenged company. The consensus among most economists would emphasize:

- the inescapable costs of any such restrictions on competition— that is to say, the inefficiencies that society incurs when it prevents the supply function from being distributed on the basis of the present marginal costs of the respective rivals;

(*...continued*)

generating—that is to say, that the generation part of the business is not a "natural monopoly"—PURPA played a substantial role in the subsequent deregulation of that part of the industry, first by inducing states to introduce mandatory acquisitions of power via competitive bids and then in the more recent comprehensive restructuring now in process in many states. See Richard F. Hirsh, *Power Loss: Technology, Regulation and the End of Consensus in the American Utility System*, MIT Press, forthcoming, Chapter 7, "PURPA, Natural Monopoly, and Market Principles."

- the encouragement that preferential subsidies and protections of this kind give to would-be competitors to devote their entrepreneurial energies primarily to seeking such preferences and ensuring their perpetuation by interventions before regulatory agencies and the courts, rather than concentrating on being more efficient suppliers than the incumbents. The U.S. experience in telecommunications regulation confirms the importance and dangers of this kind of continual rent-seeking; the current proceedings seeking to formulate codes of conduct for electric and gas utilities threaten to replicate it (See Section II.B);

- the preferability of leaving determinations of the long-term prospects of new ventures to the market, generally, and to financial markets in particular. If a new competitive venture of this kind is indeed meritorious—that is to say, carries sufficient promise of becoming profitable after an initial learning period—then the general presumption is that investors will be willing to supply the necessary capital, including the incurring of losses during the learning period. It is impossible to deny in principle the possibility that the would-be competitor may, because of the uncertainties of the market, be unable to attract that capital even for meritorious ventures. Conversely, however, to the extent that the proposed new entrant is affiliated with large enterprises, capable of marshaling the capital for such ventures, the case for governmental intervention—whether by providing seed capital or by curtailing competition and thereby imposing on consumers the cost of society's resources being used by a higher-cost entrant rather than a lower-cost incumbent—is correspondingly weakened;

- the need for a hard-headed determination of whether the would-be competitor is indeed a struggling, inexperienced newcomer that both requires and deserves some special preference in order to give it an opportunity to demonstrate its competitive merits;

- the lesson of history that, so long as companies are insulated from competition, they are, to that extent and for that reason, less likely ever to "grow up"—that is to say, attain the ability to compete without such special protections; and,

- finally, the desirability, in any event, of putting a strict limit on both the period and the extent of protection or subvention.

B. Offsetting the Advantages of Utility Company Incumbency, Legitimately and Illegitimately

One frequent refrain in the interventions by would-be competitors—whether aspiring generators and marketers of electricity; incumbent providers of local heating, air conditioning, insulation or other energy-related services faced with competition from electric and gas utilities; cable companies confronting electric company ventures into telecommunications; or long-distance telephone or cable companies opposing applications by successor Bell companies for a lifting of the prohibition, under the AT&T consent decree, of their offering interLATA or video services—is that the utility companies enjoy various competitive advantages over them that must be either offset or denied them if competition is to thrive. Most of these stem from the combining of historical public utility functions, carried over from the period of franchised monopoly, with competitive operations. Others spring from the integration, under common financial control, of competitive or potentially competitive operations with facilities to which competitors must have access on equal terms, giving rise to the possibility that the incumbents will deny them fair access or otherwise exercise that monopoly power to their unfair disadvantage or cross-subsidize their competitive operations at the expense of purchasers of monopoly services. These considerations lead, variously, to demands for the divestiture of bottleneck monopoly from competitive or potentially competitive operations, such as terminated the antitrust proceeding against AT&T, or functional separation of the entities conducting them, as in the various evolving plans for putting the control and operation of electric transmission networks under an independent system operator; and/or imposition of rules of conduct, seeking to prevent such asserted abuses of that continuing monopoly power.

Setting aside the consideration that the incumbent utility companies also are subject to unique competitive handicaps—stemming from their typically continuing obligations to extend service ubiquitously upon demand

and to cross-subsidize politically favored services and customers at the expense of others—these various threats to efficient competition are undeniable. Consequently, it is indeed an inescapable obligation of regulatory and deregulatory policy to strike the best possible balance between assuring a fair competitive opportunity to challengers and hamstringing or handicapping incumbents in the exploitation of efficiency advantages that is the essence of the socially beneficent competitive process.

I make no effort systematically to resolve all of these controversies. The ideal balance of remedial and preventive measures will clearly depend upon the context of the specific industry or markets in question and the times at which the issues are joined. In particular, while our national policy has concluded that, whatever the merits at the time of the AT&T divestiture, continuation of the categorical line-of-business restrictions on the Bell Operating Companies (BOCs) is today more anti- than pro-competitive (subject only to the tactical qualification that conditioning their lifting on the companies' cooperation in opening their local markets will further the development of competition at all levels), I do not try here to assess the case for or against continued vertical integration of electric generation, transmission, distribution and marketing.[30] At the same time, the extension of the "infant company" exception that is clearly *not* justified is the contention that rivals of the ILECs or electric utilities require some special protections or preferences merely because the incumbent companies are in a position to exploit economies that are not available to their challengers.[31]

1. Integration as a competitive phenomenon

These contentions are fallacious as a matter of both principle and fact. As for the former, competitive advantages arising out of economies of

---

[30] See, e.g., Joskow, *op. cit,*, note 8, above.

[31] See, e.g., Robert E. Hall, on behalf of MCI, *In the Matter of Application of SBC Communications Inc., et al. for Provision of In-Region, InterLata Services in Oklahoma,* before the Federal Communications Commission, CC Docket No. 97-121, *p. 55* and *passim.*

scale and scope are precisely the kind of efficiency advantages that we expect and *want* to prevail under competition. Integration is fundamentally a *competitive* phenomenon, and such efficiency advantages as it confers on the integrated firms are socially beneficent. The first fundamental competitive principle of freedom of entry means, first and foremost under conditions of real-world competition, freedom of existing firms to integrate into other operations or markets that they think they have special qualifications to serve.[32]

2. The beneficence of economies of scale and scope

Competition by integration of existing firms into related markets is most likely to be socially productive precisely because it represents an attempt to achieve the benefits of economies of scope, the manifestation of which is the ability of a firm to supply a number of products or services in combination at lower costs than if it were to supply them separately. The source of such economies is the possibility—indeed, the pervasive phenomenon—of existing firms having special capabilities (physical plant, managerial or labor forces, technological or marketing skills or reputations) of taking on the provision of additional products or services at low incremental costs.[33]

---

[32] In a book devoted to the proposition that vigorous enforcement of the antitrust laws is necessary for the preservation of fair competition, my co-author and I began the chapter "Business Integration and Monopoly" with the proposition:

> competition requires ... that business units be free, ordinarily, to take on new products, new functions, or enter new markets—in short, to integrate.

In summarizing the problem of applying the antitrust laws to the operations of integrated firms, we observed:

> The perplexing problem is that the competitive advantages stemming from gains in efficiency attributable to integration are in practice inseparable from the merely strategic advantages that pose the dangers to society just described. Efficiency gains arise from the fuller utilization of a firm's capacity, whether measured by its physical plant, managerial talents, by-products, technological skills, or the ideas issuing from its research laboratories. Dirlam and Kahn, *op. cit.*, pp. 150-51.

[33] See the similar observations in M.G. de Chazeau and A.E. Kahn, *Integration and Competition in the Petroleum Industry*, New Haven: Yale University Press, 1959, Chapter 3 and in my *The Economics of Regulation*, Vol. 2, pp. 260-261.

Among the sources of such possible economies would be:

Input sharing: The monthly utility bill typically has unused space. While there are incremental costs of computer equipment and services required to use it, lines can be added at lower costs than would be incurred in preparing and mailing an additional bill. Ratepayers are clearly no worse off for having this space utilized, because they need pay no more for billing than they were paying before; and purchasers of the non-utility services will be better off to the extent that competition among firms enjoying similar or other economies forces them to pass on those lower costs.

A local utility has a fleet of repair trucks. There are substantial costs of sending a truck out on a run from a garage. If the truck (and the service workers who go out on it) can be sent to perform more than one function, the fixed costs of the truck, transit time from the garage to the customer and personnel can be spread over more than one activity at little or no additional cost.

Electric companies are using their rights of way to install fiberoptic facilities (which also exhibit enormous economies of scale) for such internal operations as supervisory control, data acquisition, and protective relaying and to provide telecommunications services.[34]

A final example: Data processing equipment has to be sized to deal with the peak load of data to be processed. Typically, therefore, there are unused processing cycles that can be exploited at little cost. Allowing the non-utility operations to use these offpeak cycles increases efficiency in the use of the computing resources.

If such economies are present, proposals for structural separation of the services using those common facilities—and recommendations of witnesses for competitors and proposed commission rules that all such common uses of facilities or personnel be prohibited except as the services

---

[34] See the reference to 23 such ventures in note 47, below.

(or other inputs) can be transferred at published tariffs[35] and, therefore, made equally available to all applicants—would simply interfere with or totally prevent their achievement. The non-utility operation would have to employ its own trucks and personnel, its own bills and its own computers. All purchasers of its services would be hurt by such mandated separations, preventing the utility companies from taking advantage of such potential economies and passing them on, under pressure of competition—including purchasers of the regulated services, who would lose the possible benefit of sharing those savings with unregulated operations (see Section II.B.7., below).

Knowledge economies: Electric distribution companies have for years expended resources on demand side management programs. As a result certain personnel may have knowledge of the performance of innovations in heating and air conditioning and which are likely to be accepted by customers. It may be inefficient to separate those employees (or their knowledge) from the regulated firm, because they may be useful also to it.[36] Again, no ratepayer is harmed by the use of this knowledge in non-utility operations, and consumers of those unregulated services are likely to benefit.

Marketing economies: Customers typically appreciate the convenience of one-stop shopping—having a single source for both utility and non-utility services.[37] In particular, they may prefer a single bill or a single telephone

---

[35] This was the recommendation of Burnice C. Dooley, testifying on behalf of the Delaware Alliance for Fair Competition, before the Delaware Public Service Commission *Concerning the Cost Accounting Manual and Code of Conduct*, Docket No. 97-65. It is also incorporated in the *Standards of Conduct* adopted by the Massachusetts Department of Public Utilities.

[36] Such advantages need not flow from knowledge about individual customers obtained from the regulated operations and exploited exclusively by the utility companies' affiliated unregulated operations—which might be conceived of as the equivalent of an essential facility properly subject to mandatory sharing with competitors.

[37] See for example, "Study Says Consumers Would Buy Bundled Services," *Telecommunications Reports*, Aug. 12, 1996. That article reports that almost 80 percent of U.S. households would buy bundled services from a single provider. Other studies have quantified

(continued...)

number to call for help with all electricity or energy-related or telecommunications matters, from loss of service to change of supplier to advice on insulation. This integration of functions raises the possibility of utility company employees using the contacts with customers in connection with their provision of monopoly services to obtain preferential access to their patronage for competitive services.[38] On the other hand, preclusion of such a possibility by structural separation—for example, requiring separate bills, separate employee contacts, or even separate telephone numbers for the two sets of operations, in order to prevent such illegitimate steering of customers to the unregulated subsidiary—would deny customers a convenience that they value.

In this connection, there has been a great deal of argument about whether the incumbent utility companies should be permitted to attach their familiar brand names to their competitive offerings.[39] So far as the economic principle is concerned, such favorable associations as consumers may have with those brands—e.g., expectations of service quality and reliability (and certainly not all utility company brands do carry such favorable rather than hostile associations)—are an economy of scope, the benefits of which it would be anti-competitive to deny both

---

(*...continued*)

the value of "one-stop shopping" to consumers. For example, see Testimony of Arthur T. Smith on behalf of Southern Bell, Docket No. 930330-TP (Fla. P.S.C. July 1, 1994) and Timothy J. Tardiff, "The Effects of Presubscription and Other Attributes on Long-Distance Carrier Choice," *Information Economics and Policy,* Vol. 7, 1995, pp. 353-366.

[38] See Section B.4., below, recognizing that any such tying or quasi-tying might well be regarded as anticompetitive.

[39] For example, Professors R. Glenn Hubbard and William A. Lehr, in an affidavit filed on behalf of AT&T (*In the Matter of Application of SBC Communications, Inc., et al. for Provision of In Region, InterLATA Services in Oklahoma,* before the Federal Communications Commission, CC Docket No. 97-121, April 28, 1997, p. 61) cite the likely attachment by the Bell Operating Companies of their brand names to their new interLATA services, "without payment," as constituting clear "cross-subsidization"—manifestly, a loose usage of a term whose strict economic meaning is the offer of a service at rates below incremental cost, with the resulting incremental revenue deficiency being made good by other (in this context, regulated) services.

(*continued...*)

the companies and consumers who value them.[40] This value is almost certain to increase enormously over time, as residential customers, particularly, have to choose among competing suppliers of gas and electricity, where safety, reliability and continuity are likely to be aspects of the quality of service upon which they would place a high value but about which it is likely to be very difficult for them to make informed choices. In these circumstances, the several competitors are likely themselves to place heavy emphasis upon their reputations earned in other markets. The question is not, as some competitors of the utility companies have claimed, whether there may be some confusion in the minds of consumers about whether they are being served by their familiar regulated

---

(...continued)

The qualifying "without payment" attached by Professors Hubbard and Lehr to the asserted "cross-subsidization" raises the separate question of whether the ILECs should be required to reimburse purchasers of regulated services for the value of those brand names when attached to unregulated services. That issue in no way qualifies my observation that the possible benefit to the BOCs of using their familiar brands to market interLATA service is a valid economy of scope and no different in kind—or necessarily greater—than the one enjoyed by the dominant long-distance carriers in entering local markets. (Incidentally, the case for reimbursing ratepayers on the ground that they have, arguably, contributed in the past to the value of the BOC brand would seem to apply equally to AT&T.) This consideration will recur when I turn to the question of whether purchases of regulated services should share in the benefits from utility company ventures into unregulated markets, in Sections II.B.7. and III.B.

[40] See Lawrence Kaufmann, Mark Newton Lowry and David Hovde, Christensen Associates, "Branding Electric Utility Products: Analysis and Experience in Related Industries," prepared for the Edison Electric Institute, Washington, DC, August 1997, listing among the benefits of the free use of utility brands:

- brand names facilitate participation in non-core product markets, thereby spreading common costs, reducing unit costs, and making lower prices possible

- brand names promote product innovation and increase the range of non-core products available to customers

- by linking the reputation conveyed by a single name to more products, branding can increase incentives to maintain the quality of all utility company products

- brand names can provide important convenience benefits to customers

utility company or by some unregulated affiliate[41] and whether, therefore, it may be necessary to require the utility company to refrain from using its familiar brand in the competitive market. Instead, the situation is one in which it is likely to be positively *desirable* for customers to know what company is serving them and to be guided in their selection by such favorable or unfavorable experiences as they may have had with those companies in the public utility context and/or by the *reputations* of their several suitors based on their performance in other markets or providing other goods and services.[42] Comparable benefits of favorable associations (or handicaps of unfavorable associations) with their names and reputation are, of course, available to competitors—utility and non-utility, large and small, local and national.

Identical considerations apply to the asserted competitive advantage of incumbent companies stemming from their ability to add new services to their previous mix at very low incremental billing costs[43]: these are, precisely, another manifestation of the economies of scope that strongly counsel against forbidding—indeed, counsel encouraging—these companies to expand their operations into competitive markets.

---

[41] See for example, the *Recommended Decision* of the Hearing Examiner in the Delmarva case (note 35, above), Oct. 17, 1997, holding that Delmarva had violated the Public Service Commission's *Interim Code of Conduct* because its promotional activities may have caused some "confusion" of its regulated and unregulated activities—even though there was no evidence whatever that the Company had in any way linked or tied the offer of utility and non-utility services.

[42] This is in no way to deny the importance of consumers being fully apprised of when they are purchasing a regulated service from a public utility monopolist and when, instead, they have or should have an undistorted choice among competing suppliers, including the utility company itself, as I will presently re-emphasize.

[43] Many years ago, some small radiopaging companies complained to the British Office of Telecommunications Policy that the recently privatized British Telecom was competing unfairly with them because it was charging its radiopaging customers only the negligible incremental billing costs associated with adding another line to their bill, whereas the complaining competitors had to recover in their charges their much higher costs of billing for the radiopaging services alone.

OFTEL responded by requiring British Telecom to incorporate a portion of the

(*continued...*)

3. Availability of economies of scale and scope to competitors

As for the factual premise underlying arguments in favor of special protections for rivals of utility companies—namely, that comparable advantages are not available to their challengers and that the economies of scope available to the incumbents stemming from their status as franchised public utility monopolies are, therefore, likely to make efficient competition impossible—these arguments fail to take into account the principal reason why the markets for utility services have become increasingly competitive and seem likely to become so even more ubiquitously in the near future. The reason why long-distance companies such as AT&T, MCI and Sprint; cable and satellite system operators; competitive providers of access to long-distance carriers such as MFS, Teleport and Brooks Fiber; telecommunications equipment manufacturers; information and software services providers; and cellular and local electric distribution companies seek or may be expected to seek to offer or already offer local telephone and/or video services is identical in principle to the reason why the various local exchange companies (LECs) wish to offer information, video and long-

---

(*...continued*)

common billing costs in its charges for radiopaging service. I take the liberty of reproducing my comments on that decision, some 12 years ago:

> Decisions like OFTEL's in this case could result in a real sacrifice of efficiency: it would tend to transfer some radiopaging business to firms with costs higher than British Telecom's, because they do not enjoy the economy of billing for several services jointly.

OFTEL felt—perhaps correctly—that the longer-term benefits of competition outweighed such short-term efficiency losses. But attempting to preserve competition by handicapping competitors in this way is very dangerous. Typically, new entrants into deregulated industries enjoy advantages of their own sufficient to outweigh the possible advantages of incumbent firms—lower wages or overheads, greater agility or innovativeness—the very advantages that competition is supposed to bring to consumers.

As a general rule, public policy should leave the determination of whether competitors deserve to survive to the unbiased test of the market itself; and that means letting all competitors—including the incumbent companies—reflect in their prices whatever economies are available to them. (bi-weekly commentary, PBS program, *Nightly Business Report*, Nov. 8, 1985.)

For another illustration of these conflicting considerations, see note 69, below.

distance services: it is that they, too, see in these ventures the opportunity to take advantage of exactly the same kinds and sources of economies of scope,[44] including catering to the preference of consumers for purchasing all their communications services under a single billing from a single supplier.

Similarly, among the most likely challengers of incumbent local electric utility companies are the other major electric utility companies in the region with ready access to its wholesale markets via regional power pools and

---

[44] Robert Allen, then CEO of AT&T, proclaimed upon passage of the Telecommunications Reform Act in 1996:

> For business customers, he said, AT&T could use the existing direct connections between AT&T switches and many of its business customers offices to begin offering local services. Currently, a substantial number of the lines serving customers from AT&T's digital switching centers are directly connected to business customers offices, Allen said.

> He added that once the law's requirements are met by the Bell companies, AT&T need only make software adjustments and establish links to local switches in order to allow these direct connections—now used only for long distance—to handle local traffic as well.

AT&T news release, "AT&T's Allen Outlines Plans to Enter Local Telephone Market," Feb. 8, 1996.

The fact that AT&T and MCI as well have since then displayed varying degrees of enthusiasm about their previously proclaimed intention to enter into competition at the local level by employing their own facilities, as compared with concentrating their efforts on obtaining low rates for using the facilities and purchasing the local services of the ILECs for resale, does not reflect any modification of their conviction (and that of the ILECs themselves) that if they are to compete effectively, they must offer a complete package of services, local and long-distance.

As for the use of brand names and joint marketing, AT&T, of course, uses its brand for its credit card services, which it uses also as a billing mechanism for its long-distance telephone customers, its World/Net Internet service, and Direct TV, and would obviously plan to bundle local with long-distance services under that familiar identification.

In other proceedings, other expert witnesses for these companies have cited the advantage of an ILEC being able to use the same attorneys and expert witnesses as well as its bills and billing systems at very little cost to add services directly competitive with those of their clients. But anyone representing local exchange companies in regulatory proceedings, likewise, encounters the very same attorneys, company executives, and expert witnesses representing the long-distance carriers, whether the issue is the terms on which they should be enabled to purchase unbundled elements of the local exchange networks or retail services of the LECs or whether the BOCs should be permitted to enter interLATA markets in competition with them.

to retail markets when and as they obtain similar access to local distribution facilities. The number of members of the *PJM Interconnection Agreement*, for example, had swollen to 58 as of Oct. 13 1997,[45] largely in anticipation of the opening up of these markets. They are obviously not unknown, inexperienced newcomers in the generation and marketing of electric power; at least some of them have substantial excess capacity and strong incentives to mitigate their stranded costs by promoting sales out of territory. There is no more reason to handicap the local utility in meeting their competition when they invade its markets than there would be to handicap them in exploiting such economies of scope and scale as they can avail themselves of in meeting its competition as it enters their territories.

The desire to handicap one's competitors is, of course, universal. Unsurprisingly therefore, the demand for handicapping utility companies to offset their asserted advantages of scale or scope stemming from their franchised monopolies is by no means confined to cases in which rivals are attempting to challenge those historical monopolies—although it has its greatest plausibility in those circumstances. Identical arguments are used when it is the utility company that is the entrant into unregulated markets—as some electric utilities propose, for example, to enter such well-established markets as the provision of heating, ventilating, air conditioning (HVAC) and energy conserving equipment, installation and servicing,[46] as well as, in a growing number of cases, telecommuni-

---

[45] Website www.pjm.com.

[46] Here, for example, is what Professor Eleanor Craig says about the putative competitive advantages of Delmarva Power & Light in the provision of these so-called HVAC services (of which its market share is approximately 10 percent):

> The vast majority of the functions of the monopoly's unregulated affiliates have traditionally been performed in a competitive marketplace by small and medium-sized firms. For those firms to successfully compete with the monopoly utility's unregulated affiliates, they would have to be offered equal supplier deep quantity discounts, have equal name recognition and reputation and access to capital. Quite simply, the bigger monopoly-supported company could dominate the repair and service business and reduce competition in today's successful industry of largely independent contractors. By further protecting the monopoly with the rate base, the state of Delaware

(*continued...*)

cations services.[47] These demands are subject to the same fundamental criticism as I have already enunciated—on grounds of both principle and fact. It is as general "energy service companies" (ESCOs) that all these utility companies and their rivals propose to compete, *precisely* because of the economies of scale or scope that they see an opportunity to exploit in this way.

Among the more than 175 registered electric service providers in California are not only the major utility companies in the region—PG&E, Southern California Edison, PacifiCorp, Portland General Electric (now merged with Enron) and Arizona Public Service—and such other out-of-region utilities or their affiliates as the Southern Company, Dominion Resources, Duke Power, the Williams Companies, Coastal Corporation, UtiliCorp, and Central and Southwest Corp. but also affiliates of giant industrials such as Honeywell, with its dominant position in climate controls, and, via Coral Redwood, Shell Oil and Texas Gas.[48]

(*...continued*)

> would discourage new business entry, or old business expansion, and distinctly issue an unfriendly to business message for economic development.

Direct Testimony on behalf of the Delmarva Alliance for Fair Competition, in DPSC Docket No. 97-65 (note 35, above), Sept. 4, 1997, pp. 7-8.

These observations show a deplorable tendency to decry genuine efficiency advantages that firms such as Delmarva may obtain by combining unregulated with regulated operations and merely to assume, without daring explicitly to say so—let alone offering the necessary assessment of the likely competitive situation in the unregulated markets that would be affected—that the result would be monopolization of those markets by Delmarva. They also ignore Delmarva's venture into telephony, in competition with Bell Atlantic.

[47] I supply a list of 23 such ventures in my testimony on behalf of Boston Edison before the Massachusetts Department of Public Utilities in DPU 97-96 *Code of Conduct* (see note 49, below), Nov. 21, 1997, Appendix Table 2.

[48] List supplied by the Edison Electric Institute. Similarly, among the 19 companies that have already applied for licenses to sell power at retail in Pennsylvania, in competition with the Pennsylvania Power and Light Company, were not only the three other major electric utilities in the state, but also several local gas distribution companies, subsidiaries of DuPont, along with subsidiaries of out-of-state utility companies such as Houston Power and Light, Delmarva Power & Light, the Allegheny Electric Cooperative, the Southern Company, Virginia Electric Power and PacifiCorp. List supplied by PP&L.

In those several markets, it is the utility companies that would be the entrants, challenging the incumbents. The advantages the utility companies may bring to bear in the HVAC business are no different from the advantages enjoyed by Sears Roebuck and Montgomery Ward, which already provide these services in hundreds of localities, flowing from their retailing provision of a wide range of consumer goods. Local providers of heating and air-conditioning services, with whom the utilities might compete, already compete with those two giants—no doubt because they enjoy offsetting advantages of local contacts, personal service and local reputation. With regard to telecommunications, it is the electric companies that must face the entrenched monopoly incumbents—local telephone and cable companies, along with AT&T and MCI, cellular operators and manufacturers of telecommunications equipment. It is simply ludicrous to handicap the former if they enjoy efficiency advantages in providing telecommunications services that flow from their historical position as franchised providers of electric power.[49]

---

[49] Yet, as I explain in section B6, below, this is precisely what the Massachusetts standards of conduct would do, if, as that state's Department of Public Utilities is considering (as of this writing), they were to be applied to the non-energy-related affiliates of electric and gas utilities. DPU 97-96 *Code of Conduct*, Investigation initiated Oct. 17, 1997.

By an interesting—but by no means surprising—coincidence, just when the Massachusetts Department was considering this action, there appeared an article in *The Wall Street Journal* describing the mounting complaints by subscribers about the increasing rates for cable service that had occurred over the preceding year and a half. According to that article, the Federal Communications Commission had found that regulated cable systems had increased rates 8.5 percent in the 12 months ending July 4 of that year, and unregulated systems 9.6 percent:

> More troubling for policy makers, though, is what has happened since the survey was completed. In recent weeks, cable operators announced a new round of rate increases, with most taking effect next month... [T]he increases range from 7% in San Diego and Long Island, N.Y., to as much as 17% in New England.

The coincidence is to be found in this continuation of the story:

> In the few cities where there is competition, the difference in rates is striking. In Massachusetts, scheduled rate increases range from 13% to 15% in many towns. But rates haven't risen in Somerville, where competitor RCN Communications of Princeton, N.J., began building a cable system. And in parts of Boston, where RCN also offers service, rate increases were only 2.5%.

(continued...)

4. The legitimate need for antitrust-like protections

None of these reservations I have expressed about the demands by challengers for elimination of the advantages of incumbency is intended to minimize their legitimate demands for competitive parity as it would be defined under the antitrust laws. As I have pointed out, regulatory intervention of some kind is necessary to ensure equality of access to essential facilities controlled by the incumbent companies and protection from utility company competition truly cross-subsidized at the expense of monopoly services or uses in other ways of public utility monopolies to illegitimately favor competitive affiliates. Examples of the latter practices would be tying the provision of utility services to the competitive offerings of affiliates (for example, by offering more favorable terms for the former) or, even more modestly, using the occasion of contacts with customers (via phone or service calls) stemming from providing them utility service to bias their choices between the company's unregulated offerings and those of their competitors.[49a] Just as efficient competition must be conducted on the basis of the relative efficiencies of the several

---

(...*continued*)

"FCC Balks At Freezing Cable Rates," *The Wall Street Journal,* Dec. 17, 1997, pp. A3, 6. RCN BecoCom is a joint venture of Boston Edison and a small competitive local exchange service provider.

Cable companies have typically defended these recent increases on the ground that they have been associated with enriched programming and additional channels; I have no basis for questioning those assertions. The difference between the behavior of rates in the territory RCN then served and in the rest of the country is nevertheless eloquent testimony to the benefits of the competition that the Massachusetts standards of conduct would inexcusably handicap.

[49a] I am uncertain how strict the prohibition of "steering" customers from utility to non-utility services on such occasions should be. Presumably it should be strictly applied to local distribution companies' sales of monopoly services—i.e., the electric power itself—in their franchise territories. It could well be anti-competitive, on balance, however, if they or their employees were flatly prohibited from promoting new, unregulated services in such situations—where customers were well aware of the availability of competing suppliers—so long as there was no hint of anti-competitive tying. As for the enforceability of prohibitions of illicit steering, it should not be difficult to ascertain, by anonymous spot checking, whether companies are violating rules prohibiting such tactics.

contenders, so also must it be unbiased by the exercise of monopoly power to exclude rivals from the opportunity to compete on that same basis.

Arguably, this function might be left to the antitrust laws. But protection of captive ratepayers remains the continuing responsibility of regulatory commissions. The fact that it is the possibility of costs causally attributable to the competitive operations being shifted to captive purchasers of the monopoly services that makes cross-subsidization a particular, if not unique, possibility in the public utility industries inevitably confers on regulatory agencies the primary responsibility for preventing it on a continuing basis.[49b] Finally, determination and enforcement of the terms of fair access to essential facilities is so clearly regulatory in nature, it is unlikely to be effectively performed by the courts.[50]

Historically, however, regulatory commissions have shown a systematic tendency to go well beyond ensuring challengers of monopoly telephone companies a fair opportunity to compete on the basis of their relative efficiency—protecting them from cross-subsidized predation or vertical squeezes and ensuring them access on equal terms to essential facilities controlled by the incumbents—by extending preferences unrelated to their efficiency and protecting them from efficient competitive responses by the incumbent firms.

[49b] Companies in unregulated industries are from time to time accused of engaging in that same practice. For an unregulated company to attempt to recoup losses of revenue consequent on price reductions in competitive markets by raising others of its prices would make sense, however, only if it had previously not been setting the latter prices at profit –maximizing levels and was somehow induced by its competitive price reductions to correct that irrationality. It is only under regulation that sellers are systematically prevented from fully exploiting their monopoly power in the prices they are permitted to charge their captive customers and may then be enabled to come closer to doing so if losses on the sale of competitive services help them persuade regulators to permit it, in order to restore their overall rates of return or if they can shift costs from competitive to regulated operations—thereby completing the circle of *cross*-subsidization.

[50] For a survey of experience confirming this conclusion see Pablo T. Spiller and Carlo G. Cardilli, "The Frontier of Telecommunications Deregulation: Small Countries Leading the Pack," *Journal of Economic Perspectives*, Vol. 11, No. 4 (Fall 1997), pp. 127-38.

The most extreme of these protections has been the line of business restrictions imposed on the severed Bell Operating Companies under the
Modified Final Judgment (MFJ) that terminated the AT&T antitrust
case. It would, of course, be a distortion to characterize those restrictions as flatly anti-competitive: the purpose was, by totally separating
the putatively naturally monopolistic local telephone service from the
other potentially more competitive services—in particular, long-
distance—to remove from the local Bell companies both the power and
the incentive to exclude rivals from a fair opportunity to compete. What
ultimately resolved the debate over the many years leading up to the
MFJ on the side of divestiture and flat prohibitions was the developing
view of the Department of Justice that all the proposed alternative protections against these practices would be excessively regulatory and in-
effective and only a total separation would be consistent with the
preservation and promotion of competition in the other markets.[51]

At the same time, it is also undeniable that such flat prohibitions—seeking as they do to protect *competition* by prohibiting one party, typically
the one in the best position to compete vigorously, from competing *at
all*—are themselves inherently anti-competitive. What stands out most
clearly from the complex history leading up to the AT&T dissolution is
that, however widely the contesting parties differed in their assessments
of the terms of the trade-off between preservation of the benefits of the
vertical and horizontal integration of the Bell System, on the one side,
and securing the maximum protections against exclusionary practices
by AT&T, on the other, and however extreme the final resolution, both
parties recognized that there was a conflict between the two goals and
that the final resolution did involve sacrificing some benefits of integration—i.e., economies of scope.[52]

---

[51] A particularly thorough history of these debates is presented by Peter Temin, *The
Fall of the Bell System, A Study in Crisis and Politics*, New York: Cambridge
University Press, 1987.

[52] Ironically, Assistant Attorney General William F. Baxter, who almost single-handedly
kept the Reagan Administration on the divestiture track, in the face of opposition by
higher and in all other respects more powerful members of the Administration, has
consistently been a forthright exponent of the proposition that vertical integration

(*continued...*)

The second competitive handicapping of the local exchange companies, which continues to this day, is that their services must be offered only under open tariffs, subject to prior regulatory approval. This require- ment gives competitors advance notice of what is coming and a legal op- portunity to delay its introduction by intervening in opposition before the regulatory commission while preparing their own market re- sponses—indeed, to "respond" before the LECs are permitted to release a competitive initiative to the market.

Third, LECs are still, at both the local and national levels, subject to re- quired systemwide averaging of costs and prices, with consequent exposure to competitive undercutting in low-cost markets. At the same time, they are required, as carriers of last resort, to serve high-cost markets at non- compensatory rates. And their proposed competitive rates have been tested against a standard derived from full allocations of costs consisting very largely of economically meaningless carrying costs of investments at historic, net book values that have only the remotest relationship to current market values and costs.[53]

(*...continued*)

　(in unregulated industries) is not a proper subject of attack under the antitrust laws—that it not only poses no threat to competition but is positively beneficial. Absent regulation, he has contended, vertical integration (a) cannot in itself en- hance or extend monopoly and (b) is likely to conduce to improved efficiency. See his "The Viability of Vertical Restraints Doctrine," *California Law Review*, Vol. 75, No. 3, May 1987, pp. 933-950 and statement before the Subcommittee on Telecommunications, U.S. House of Representatives, March 10, 1982, mimeo ver- sion, pp. 2-3. Several years after the event, confronted with the question of whether "there were lots of scope economies" sacrificed by the decree, the then-Professor Baxter responded:

　　then the decree looks less wise than it would in the contrary situation. The decree implicitly made a wager that the regulatory distortions of those portions of the econ- omy, which could have been workably competitive, yielded social losses in excess of the magnitude of economies of scope that would be sacrificed by this approach. It was a wager, a guess.... It was a judgment call, and I guess, in some senses, I do not yet know. Maybe we will never know whether it was right or wrong.

　Barry G. Cole (ed.), *After the Breakup: Assessing the New Post-AT&T Divestiture Era*, New York: Columbia University Press, 1991, p. 30.

[53] For a demonstration of the economic irrelevancy and inefficiency of price floors based on such fully allocated costs, see William J. Baumol, Michael F. Koehn and

(*continued...*)

5. Preserving competition vs. protecting competitors

Whatever one's evaluation of these asymmetrical restraints upon the competitive initiatives and responses of the incumbent companies, there can be no doubt that in essential respects they go beyond the mere preservation of competition in the direction of protecting *competitors from* competition—effectively imposing regimes of cartelization on potentially competitive markets.[54]

By a poignant historical coincidence, AT&T—which continues to oppose attempts by the local exchange companies to be freed from these asymmetrical regulatory impediments bearing only on themselves and handicapping them in competing with challengers—has itself been the strongest proponent of the "level playing field" that they seek. It spelled out its criticisms of this kind of regulation in eloquent detail back in 1983, in FCC proceedings *In the Matter of Long-Run Regulation of AT&T's Basic Domestic Interstate Services*—most persuasively in a statement by Professor Richard Schmalensee:

(*...continued*)

Robert D. Willig, "How Arbitrary is 'Arbitrary'?—or, Toward The Deserved Demise of Full Cost Allocation," *Public Utilities Fortnightly*, Sept. 3, 1987, pp. 16-21, and my own "The Uneasy Marriage of Regulation and Competition," *Telematics*, Vol. 1, No. 5, September 1984, p. 12, and my *The Economics of Regulation*, summarizing and analyzing the controversies flowing from the Federal Communications Commission's Seven-Way Cost Study, with economic experts representing AT&T proclaiming the principle, unexceptionable in itself, that the only price floors consistent with economic efficiency would be long-run incremental costs and opponents—defenders of the FCC's study—reiterating their fears of cross-subsidization, illicit shifting of AT&T's costs from competitive to monopoly services and the like. Vol. 1, pp. 152-158, Vol. 2, p. 152n.

The ILECs were once handicapped quite generally by the requirement that their proposed construction of new facilities be certified by their regulatory commissions, with similar consequences in terms of the possibilities of delay and impairment of their ability to compete. Some states have dropped that obligation, as a logical accompaniment to substituting price caps for rate base/rate of return regulation.

[54] Professors William J. Baumol, Otto Eckstein and I, constituting AT&T's Economic Advisory Council, prepared a memorandum published by the company, dated Nov. 23, 1970, on the subject "Competition and Monopoly in Telecommunication Services,"

(*continued...*)

The social costs of asymmetric regulation of AT&T's provision of telecommunications services include all the direct, administrative costs of that regulation borne by AT&T, the Commission, AT&T's rivals, and other parties. AT&T bears a differential burden here because it must comply with regulatory requirements from which its rivals have been largely exempted. Moreover, as competition becomes more vigorous and the marketplace becomes more dynamic, AT&T will need to change prices and products more frequently in order to remain competitive. Under the current policy of asymmetric regulation, this will result in more frequent filings with the Commission, and AT&T's differential burden will become more severe.

While the administrative costs of asymmetric regulation are substantial and will grow rapidly as competition intensifies, the most important costs imposed on AT&T and on society as a whole by the current regulatory policy in telecommunications services are not administrative. More important, though perhaps less visible, are the indirect costs that arise from the handicaps and perverse incentives inevitably created by conventional regulation in the presence of competition...

(*...continued*)

the central argument of which was that of the four possible regimes for telecommunications—"regulated monopoly," "full competition with guarantees to prevent abuses," "full competition in only certain segments of the market," and "'competitors' protected from full competition"—(p. 2) the last of these was the worst of all:

> This kind of government-enforced cartelization and division of markets can result in tremendous inefficiency and prove very costly to the body of consumers whose interests the Commission decides to protect. (p. 13)

> [I]n short, if full competition is not to be sham firms already in the field must be permitted to compete fully with new entrants and the pressures of the market must be left to determine the victors (pp. 8-9)

—all of these, manifestly, positions totally congenial to AT&T itself.

> As I later put it independently, after direct involvement in a regime of cartelization-by-regulation:

> The regulator tends as a matter of constitutional preference ... to convert the maintaining of the 'level playing fields' into an interference with the contest itself. Regulators move from trying to assure a fair and equal start to ensuring an equal finish; to preserve whatever the regulator conceives to be the proper market shares of the various competitors.

(*continued...*)

The many differential regulatory burdens discussed above prevent AT&T from using all its substantial assets, both human and tangible, effectively in the competitive arena to meet customer needs. Regulation inevitably reduces incentives to produce efficiently and to innovate vigorously. [footnote omitted] It does this directly by limiting the allowed returns from efficiency and innovation and indirectly by imposing delays and rigidities that reduce possible returns. Regulation-induced distortions in pricing distort carrier-specific and market-wide demand patterns and thus distort the utilization of existing capacity. While pricing distortions may benefit some competitors and users, society as a whole loses. Society also loses if AT&T's incentives to deliver services at minimum cost are dulled, so that its costs are higher than they should be.[55]

AT&T essentially repeated these arguments 12 years later in its at last successful motion to be reclassified as a non-dominant carrier. As the FCC summarized its argument:

AT&T argues that continuing to regulate it as a dominant carrier imposes direct costs on carriers and customers, and does not facilitate a competitive market for interstate, domestic, interexchange services.

(*...continued*)

In short, regulation confronted with competition will have a systematic tendency either to suppress it ... or to orchestrate it and control the results it produces ....

Specifically, we are going to find regulatory commissions actively and continuously engaged, consciously or unconsciously, in handicapping the Bell companies, hampering their efforts genuinely to compete, in the interest of protecting both competitors and captive customers from the respective burdens of cross-subsidization.

"The Uneasy Marriage of Regulation and Competition," *loc. cit.*, pp. 9, 11. See also John Haring, "The FCC, the OCCs and the Exploitation of Affection," Federal Communications Commission, Office of Plans and Policy Working Paper Series, No. 17 (June 1985), whose central thesis is that new competitors can exploit the "personal stake" "that government decision makers have ... in the success of the policies they pursue, in the instant [*sic*] setting policies designed to promote competition in the long-distance business ... by threatening to fail"—and in this way elicit policies that protect them from competition. (p. 13) .

[55] CC Docket No. 83-1147, Attachment 4, Attachments and Appendices to Comments of American Telephone And Telegraph Company, pp. 10-11, 18-19.

AT&T claims that, despite loss of market power, it continues to be subjected to 'burdensome and unequal' regulation that unfairly advantages its competitors and deprives consumers of price reductions and innovative service offerings.[56]

The FCC agreed:

The cost of dominant carrier regulation of AT&T in this context includes inhibiting AT&T from quickly introducing new services and from quickly responding to new offerings by its rivals. This occurs because of the longer tariff notice requirements imposed on AT&T, which allow AT&T's competitors to respond to AT&T tariff filings covering new services and promotions even before AT&T's tariffs become effective.... Furthermore, such regulation imposes compliance costs on AT&T and administrative costs on the Commission.[57]

... We believe that, in such a situation, the costs of continuing to subject all of AT&T's interstate, domestic, interexchange services to dominant carrier regulation, outweigh the benefits of that regulation.[58]

6. Electric and gas utility codes of conduct

The unhappy fact is that the "codes [or standards] of conduct" now being developed in the several regulatory jurisdictions, as they proceed to open the electric and gas utilities to competition, threaten to repeat this history. Of course, as I have already made clear, the case for handicapping incumbents and protecting challengers cannot be rejected out of hand. What is shocking about these evolving codes, however, is that the handicaps are being proposed—and imposed—without any evidence of

---

[56] *Order, In the Matter of Motion of AT&T Corp. to be Reclassified as a Non-Dominant Carrier*, CC Docket No. 95-427, Adopted Oct. 12, 1995, par. 16 (footnote omitted).

[57] *Ibid.*, par. 27.

[58] *Ibid.*, par. 33.

the prerequisite searching assessment of the specific circumstances in the markets in question, including, prominently, careful consideration of whether rivals of the incumbent utilities may enjoy similar or offsetting economies or competitive advantages. In the absence of such an assessment, there is no substitute for seeing whether competition does in fact succeed rather than assuming it will not. The burden of proof that unfettered competition will not succeed should rest with those who propose restrictions that would sacrifice these efficiencies and, thereby, suppress competition between the incumbent and its rivals based on them.

For example, the *Standards of Conduct* already adopted by the Massachusetts Department of Public Utilities provide that

> (4) If a Distribution Company provides an Affiliated Company, or a customer of an Affiliated Company, any product or service other than general and administrative support services, it shall make the same products or services available to all Non-affiliated Suppliers, or customers of Non-affiliated Suppliers, on a non-discriminatory basis.

> (6) If a Distribution Company offers an Affiliated Company, or a customer of an Affiliated Company, a discount, rebate or fee waiver for *any product or service*, it shall make the same discount, rebate or fee waiver available to all Non-affiliated Suppliers, or customers of Non-affiliated Suppliers, on a non-discriminatory basis.

> (13) Employees of a Distribution Company shall not be shared with an Affiliated Company, and shall be physically separated from those of the Affiliated Company.[59]

And the California affiliate transactions rules[59a] explicitly prohibit sharing by the utilities and unregulated affiliates of office space, office equipment, office services or systems and computer and information systems except in the performance of shared corporate support functions.

---

[59] 220 C.M.R. §§ 12.03, pars. 4, 6, 13 (stress supplied). There are similar provisions in the proposed California rules.

[59a] *Decision* 97-12-088, *Rulemaking* 97-04-011, Dec. 16, 1997.

Observe that these rules apply not only—unobjectionably—to *tariffed utility services*; they would also prohibit the sharing by utility companies and their affiliates of such facilities and *non-tariffed* products and services as procurement, fiberoptic transmission, trucks, bills, employees and computing facilities, either explicitly or by attaching a condition of equivalent sharing with competitors that may well be infeasible to comply with. The principles of efficient competition in industry generally certainly do not require companies, as the rules put it, to make all such inputs "available on a non-discriminatory basis to all Non-affiliated Suppliers transacting business in [their] service territory," except if and as those inputs are genuinely *essential facilities*—that is, they cannot be duplicated elsewhere and competitors must have access to them in order to have a fair opportunity to compete on the basis of their efficiency.

Moreover, these restrictions apply not merely to activities of the incumbent companies in the markets in which they have a monopoly—the local distribution of gas and electricity—but, in total inversion of the infant industry rationale, markets, such as heating, ventilating, air conditioning and telecommunications, in which they have only minority shares or that they are proposing to enter for the first time.[60]

On the other hand, it is important to distinguish the two purposes of rules such as these, even though they are often not differentiated by their proponents and are typically both rationalized in terms of the asserted "unfairness" of competitive advantages stemming from the combining of historical franchised monopoly and newly competitive activities. One is, explicitly or by imposing impracticable conditions, to deny utility companies the opportunity to exploit genuine economies of scale or scope; the other is to offer equal access to those economies to non-affiliated competitors.

---

[60] The Massachusetts Department is, as of this writing, merely *considering* whether these same standards—already applicable to affiliates engaged in energy-related markets—should be applicable also to the activities of the electric and gas utilities in non-energy-related markets, such as telecommunications, where their application would be simply ridiculous. See note 49, above.

The first purpose is clearly protectionist and inefficient. The second is in principle unexceptionable: where the advantage stems not from any particular enterprise or innovation on the part of the utility company but merely from its having enjoyed a franchised monopoly, there is no reason for it to have exclusive enjoyment of those economies and every reason, in the interest of efficient competition, to make them available to competitors. For example, Illinois requires utility companies to bill on behalf of non-affiliated competitors on the same terms as their unregulated affiliates. Distribution companies send out bills as part of their franchised monopoly operations; the possibility of using them to bill for energy sales by unregulated affiliates, at low incremental cost, creates an opportunity for economies that there is no reason to confine to those affiliates.

On the other hand, the feasibility of such sharing will vary widely from one possible source of such an economy to another; and, therefore, as I have already suggested, prohibitions of sharing with affiliates except if the same opportunities are offered to outsiders on the same terms and conditions are likely to amount, in many if not most cases, to an inefficient flat prohibition.

The reason businesses conduct a number of operations under the umbrella of a single financially affiliated entity, rather than through market transactions, is, in a fundamental sense, the belief that subjection of these several operations to unitary managerial control permits the achievement of savings of transactions costs, as well as avoiding the uncertainties of trying to achieve the requisite coordination by purchases and sales in the market.[60a] In these circumstances, the very notion of requiring a firm to share those economies "equally" with outsiders contradicts the very notion of a firm: what would it mean to require a utility company, if it is to share computing facilities, workers, procurement, office space and experience in offering both electric power distribution and the energy itself (along with energy-related services) in the competitive

---

[60a] Ronald Coase, "The Nature of the Firm," *Economica, Vol.* 4 (1937), pp. 386-405; Oliver Williamson, "Transaction-Cost Economics: The Governance of Contractual Relations," *Journal of Law and Economics*, Vol. 22 (1979), pp. 233-261.

market, to "share" them also with outsiders? If it tried to sell these "shared resources" to non-affiliates, the transactions cost of doing so would almost certainly eat up the difference between their incremental cost and market value: if that were not so, there would have been no point conducting the several operations instead within the firm. These are economies specific to the integrated nature of the utility company and its affiliate: we rarely see firms in competitive markets renting out employees or equipment or experience to others for short periods of time. And if, for these reasons, it costs more for a utility company to make inputs available to rivals than to its own unregulated affiliates, efficiency requires that the competitors pay correspondingly higher prices than the affiliates, just as in the case of the access fees that local telephone companies charge their competitors (see note 80, below)—"infant company" considerations aside.

7. The asserted entitlement of utility ratepayers to compensation

The demands of competitors for protection against utility companies' exploitation of economies of scale and scope merge with assertions by them—with the enthusiastic support of some commission staffs and public interest intervenors—that purchasers of utility services are entitled not merely to protection against being made to bear the brunt of cross-subsidization of competitive operations but also to some compensation or sharing in the benefits of those operations.[61] The solicitude expressed by competitors for the interests of the purchasers of regulated services is of course totally self-interested: the more the utility companies' unregulated ventures are burdened with such compensations, the less their competitive threat. It is possible also to dismiss as simply erroneous the frequent contentions of these various parties that transfers of inputs—personnel, facilities, materials and equipment—from utility to non-utility operations at bare incremental costs constitutes cross-subsidization. So long as the former operations are compensated for those incremental costs, there can be no cross-subsidy or burden on utility ratepayers.

---

[61] See the critical reference to a local telephone company's attaching its brand to the offer of interLATA services, "without payment," in note 39, above.

On the other hand, the proper distribution between regulated and unregulated operations of the benefits of such economies of scale and scope, which cause incremental costs to be lower than stand-alone costs, is a legitimate issue, to which we turn in Section III.B.

C. The Resolution of the Telecommunications Act

The Telecommunications Act of 1996 represents the definitive abandonment of the categorical line-of-business restrictions on the BOCs and a return to reliance on regulatory restraints and obligations of all LECs to permit a simultaneous opening of the local markets to effective competition, on the one side, and interLATA entry by the BOCs, on the other. It would accomplish this by requiring the LECs to

- make unbundled portions of their facilities—especially the costly access lines that connect their switches with customers— available to their competitors at cost plus a "reasonable profit," in consideration of the likelihood that total competitive duplication of their facilities would be inefficient, and

- make all their retail services available to competitors for resale at discounts from their retail prices equivalent to their own avoided costs—an explicit application of the efficient component pricing rule.

I will later criticize some of the subsequent interpretations of these provisions, particularly by the FCC, but point out at once that the regulatory protections afforded competitors by these obligations imposed on ILECs by the governing statutes and regulatory policies go far beyond what would be called for under standard antitrust doctrine. Requiring incumbent monopolists to make available to competitors at something close to bare cost not merely genuinely essential facilities under their control but all network elements "for which it is technically feasible to provide access on an unbundled basis[62]—indeed, virtually any and all

---

[62] FCC, *First Report and Order, In the Matter of Implementation of the Local Competition Provisions in the Telecommunications Act of 1996, CC Docket No. 96-98, Aug. 1, 1996* (hereinafter, *Interconnection Order*), par. 278.

possible sources of competitive advantage, past, present and future, including advantages that they may develop by their own enterprise and innovation[63]—threatens to run afoul of the other important concern of antitrust policy—namely, that even firms with monopoly power not be denied the benefit of competitive advantages stemming from superior enterprise or innovation or superior efficiency, whatever its source, and their incentives to compete vigorously not be impaired.[64] For this reason, they in a very real sense discourage competition itself, in the name of encouraging it: if potential competitors can obtain from incumbents, at regulatorily-prescribed prices, not just facilities and services that are naturally monopolistic but any and all others—present and future—that could feasibly be supplied independently, the incentive of incumbents to innovate and of competitors to provide their own will be attenuated.

On the other hand, the historical monopolies of the local telephone (or electric or gas) utilities can hardly be said to have been "thrust upon them" by their "superior skill, foresight and industry." For this reason, as I have already pointed out, it may be perfectly reasonable—and conducive to efficient competition—to require them to share with competitors economies

---

[63] The antitrust laws attempt to confine the "essential facilities" obligation to truly monopoly inputs for which competitors have no feasible alternatives (see, for example, Baumol and Sidak, *Toward Competition in Local Telephony*, Cambridge: The MIT Press, 1994, p. 93); and they attempt, correspondingly, <u>not</u> to require that "the economies of density, connectivity, and scale" of incumbents or even dominant firms "be shared with entrants" (*Interconnection Order,* par. 11), without regard to whether the rivals may have corresponding or offsetting economies of scale or scope of their own—as such would-be rivals of the ILECs as the long-distance, cable or electric companies and competitive dialtone providers in metropolitan areas clearly have.

As the late Professor Philip Areeda, a leading antitrust authority, observed:

There is no general duty to share. Compulsory access, if it exists at all, is and should be very exceptional .... No one should be forced to deal unless doing so is likely substantially to improve competition in the marketplace .... ("Essential Facilities: An Epithet in Need of Limiting Principles," *Antitrust Law Journal,* Vol. 58, 1990, pp. 841-853)

[64] "[T]he successful competitor, having been urged to compete, must not be turned upon when he wins ...." (*U.S. v. Aluminum Co. of America,* 148 F. 2d. 416, 430, 1945). This decision also contains the admonition against a monopoly being condemned if the monopoly power was "thrust upon" its possessor, or if one company had survived by virtue of its "superior skill, foresight, and industry." (*Ibid.,* 429-430.)

stemming from the combining of monopoly with competitive activities, to the extent such sharing is feasible. And undoing those inherited monopolies may indeed require remedies such as the antitrust laws would apply only in extreme cases of monopolization.[65]

The logic of the sales for resale obligation on the LECs is similar to the requirement that they make unbundled parts of their networks or network elements available to competitors. Particularly where, as it appears, competition will take the form very largely of rivals offering customers complete bundles of services—local, toll, video, internet access—competitive entrants are likely to be severely handicapped if they must provide such full packages exclusively through their own efforts. The expectation is, therefore, that if they are to be able to compete effectively, they will have to be ensured the opportunity to round out their offerings by supplementing such packages as they are able to provide using their own facilities, or facilities leased from the incumbents, with retail services purchased from the LECs at wholesale discounts sufficient to enable them to compete if they are equally efficient in performing the retail function.

But neither the Act nor the FCC's rules contains any limitation on the right of entrants to demand unbundled elements or retail services designed to ensure that they merely *supplement* what the rivals can provide with their own efforts or, even worse, any provision for phasing out this invitation to a free ride on the facilities and offerings of the incumbents at regulatorily prescribed discounts. On the contrary, it enables them, at the extreme, to operate as pure resellers, indefinitely, with the ability to demand from the incumbents not only such retail services or packages

---

[65] The antitrust laws do not condemn monopoly—i.e., the possession of monopoly power—as such; what they prohibit is "monopolizing"—i.e., the achievement or perpetuation of monopoly power by "artificial" means—combinations, conspiracies or exclusionary practices that deny equally or potentially equally efficient rivals a fair opportunity to compete. See my "Standards for Antitrust Policy," *Harvard Law Review*, Volume 67, November 1953, pp. 28-54. For an excellent exposition of the logic behind the Telecommunications Reform Act and of the FCC's *Interconnection Order*, see Ingo Vogelsang and Bridger M. Mitchell, *Telecommunications Competition, the Last Ten Miles*, Cambridge: MIT Press, 1997, chapters 8 and 10.

as the latter companies offer directly to their own customers *today* but any and all future offerings or promotions of more than 90 days— at prescribed wholesale discounts in something like the 17-25 percent range now "suggested" by the Commission and adopted widely by the states.[66] I am unaware of any precedent in the antitrust laws for such a wholesale requirement—no doubt because it would tend to discourage competition itself.[67]

---

[66] On the reasonableness of those prescribed discounts, see III C 2, below.

[67] In a proceeding on a reorganization proposal of the Southern New England Telephone Company (SNET), under which, among other things, its unregulated retailing subsidiary would be free of such a sales-for-resale obligation (while its regulated wholesale subsidiary would continue to be subject to such an obligation, but only with respect to SNET retail services as of the effective date of the proposed reorganization and at the prices prevailing at that time), AT&T denied that application of the Telecommunications Act's resale obligations on the proposed retail subsidiary would constitute an impediment to competitive innovation, citing the fact that it had itself long been subject to just such an obligation:

> To jump start competition in the interexchange marketplace, the FCC ordered AT&T to offer its services for resale at discounts. AT&T's long-distance services have been offered for resale for at least ten years. This has not precluded AT&T from offering innovative, long-distance services, such as AT&T One Rate. In fact, the long-distance marketplace is now characterized by its abundance of innovative competitive offers...

(Comments of AT&T Communications of New England, Inc., March 10, 1997, p. 15, in State of Connecticut Department of Public Utility Control, Docket No. 94-10-05, *Investigation of the Southern New England Telephone Company Affiliate Matters Associated with the Implementation of Public Act 94-83.*)

Its analogy is a masterpiece of irrelevance. Under the FCC's rules, AT&T was ordered to cease denying resellers the right to purchase its services *at its own chosen retail rates.* Those rates often reflected large discounts to big customers, which offered an opportunity for arbitrage if resellers could obtain them. The rules told AT&T it could not lawfully deny *those same discounted retail* rates to resellers who would in all other respects have qualified for them. Under SNET's proposal, its unregulated retail subsidiary would continue to be subject to this obligation, as would all other common carriers. What SNET sought, instead, was freedom from any requirement to make its *future* retail offerings available to competitors at its own retail rates *minus the 17.8 percent discount* that the Connecticut Department had prescribed. For example, AT&T at the time was offering customers a 5 cents per minute rate for intraLATA toll service. Under the resale obligations to which it was subject, it would have had to permit resellers to buy that service from it at that same

(*continued...*)

The asymmetrical imposition on incumbent firms of the obligation to share with competitors at prescribed discounts all service and marketing offerings and innovations, both present and future, may or may not be justified by the logic of "infant company" considerations, as a transitional expedient. Clearly, however—just as categorical prohibitions on incumbent firms offering particular services or denying them the right to fully reflect economies of scope in their pricing of competitive services or requiring them to share with competitors any or all sources of such competitive advantages as they may develop in the future—it conflicts in fundamental ways with the dictates of competition.[68]

(...*continued*)

rate. If SNET's retail affiliate sought to match that price and AT&T's view were to prevail, it would have to offer that same retail service to competitors—including AT&T—at 4.11 cents a minute! It takes little imagination to see how such an obligation, imposed on the incumbent telephone company but not its rivals, would limit its ability to compete with them: it would obviously dampen its incentive to offer new promotions if, whatever their nature and level, it would have to offer them also to its competitors at a 17.8 percent discount.

As an astute Canadian participant in similar deregulation proceedings has observed, rhetorically:

imagine MCI being able to demand that each minute of long distance traffic be sold to it at a guaranteed discount and that if AT&T lowered the retail price, the price to MCI would automatically go down.

Willie Grieve, "Competition and Regulation in Deregulated Industries," unpublished presentation to the London Business School, London, England, June 17, 1997.

[68] In the midst of a familiar but unexceptionable recital of the prospective benefits of competition, David L. Kaserman and John W. Mayo attribute similar benefits to "the establishment of an efficient regulatorily determined wholesale price." "An Efficient Avoided Cost Pricing Rule for Resale of Local Exchange Telephone Services," *Journal of Regulatory Economics*, Vol. 11, pp. 91-107 (1997). That translation is glib. The purported benefits they cite fall under three headings:

(1) prescription of a wholesale margin will "act as a pure price cap to sustain incentives for the incumbent facilities-based provider to engage in cost-reducing innovation";

(2) by dissipating the monopoly power of the incumbents, it offers the prospect of permitting "massive reductions in the regulatory bureaucracy and the costs that are associated with it"; and

(*continued...*)

The result is a continuing tension between the regulatory interventions necessary to ensure entrants a fair *opportunity* to compete and an understandable inclination to go farther and protect challengers—at least on a

---

(*...continued*)

> (3) "as new competitors enter the local exchange arena, incumbent firms will be pressed to introduce new and innovative services ...." p. 92, note 3.

In these several arguments, they fail to observe the difference in the likely effects of the mandatory sales for resale provisions of the Act, which encourage competitive *retailing* only, and the other provisions encouraging competition at the *wholesale* level—indeed, the likely conflict between the two, as the ubiquitous availability of the resale option, at inefficiently generous rates (see Section III.C.2., below), discourages the latter form of competition.

As for the first asserted benefit, their exposition ignores the fact that the "efficient wholesale price" to which they refer is not that at all, since it says nothing about the absolute level of that "wholesale price," but, rather, a putatively efficient fixed *discount* from the retail price of the ILECs. (Their proposal would include in the discount any "excess profits" and the costs of ILEC inefficiencies at the retail stage, with the avowed intention of setting the price itself at an efficient level. Entirely apart from the vacuity of the concept of "profit" as applied to a single product of a multi-product firm, however, they offer no suggestion of how they would measure it. And while their prescription would in principle eliminate X-efficiencies in the performance of the *retail* function, by—very sensibly, as I will argue in Section III.C.2—equating the wholesale discount to the actual avoided costs of the incumbent, rather than the hypothetical costs of an ideally efficient competitor, that would still leave consumers bearing the burden of such inefficiencies and "excess profits" at all but the retail levels.) So regulation would in principle continue to be necessary.

Suppose, then, first, that the retail price is regulated, as most of them still are. In these circumstances, it is the cap on the retail prices—and the corresponding cap on the wholesale prices consequent on the prescribed discount—that provides incentives of the ILECs to efficient performance. The reselling provision adds nothing to the incentive effects of the former.

Suppose, instead, the retail price is not regulated. In these circumstances, the resale provision can only (a) discourage ILECs from reducing their prices, since they will have to pass the reduction on at the wholesale level to resellers, and (b) discourage facilities-based competition at the wholesale level. I fail to see how these effects would put pressure on the incumbents to improve their efficiency.

As for the second asserted benefit—the promise that an "efficient regulatorily-determined wholesale price" offers to reduce the need for regulation:

- it still requires that same "regulatory bureaucracy" to set the "efficient wholesale discount";

(*continued...*)

transitional basis—from disadvantages stemming from superior efficiencies enjoyed by the incumbents because of their inherited monopolies,[69] superior enterprise, innovation, or luck.

(...*continued*)

- it not only does nothing to abate monopoly-sheltered inefficiencies in the provision of the services at wholesale, which is the primary occasion for regulation, but

- it *discourages* the alternative of competition in the provision of the services themselves at the wholesale level, which would indeed make deregulation possible.

Apart from its effect—which I have, of course, conceded—of facilitating the entry of CLECs into competition at the wholesale level, by enabling them to round out their service offerings, therefore, I cannot see that the reselling provisions of the Act do *anything* to diminish the need for regulation.

Similar reservations apply to the third benefit they adduce:

- As I will proceed to observe, if the ILECs have to share their innovations with resellers at prescribed discounts, this surely weakens rather than intensifies their incentives to innovate; and

- the availability of the option of reselling the services of the ILECs at guaranteed wholesale discounts surely discourages innovation by the CLECs as well.

[69] An outstanding illustration of this tendency, protectionist of competitors, is the continuing requirement by the FCC that the access charges by LECs be the same for all long-distance carriers on a minutes-of-use basis, thereby denying the larger long-distance carriers the opportunity to obtain discounts reflecting the cost savings achievable by virtue of the large volume of their purchases of that service. The provision was understandable as a transitional measure. If challengers of AT&T were in all other respects actually or potentially equally efficient—i.e., except for their having to purchase their access services in smaller volume or at the LEC's tandem switch rather than at an end office—they might never be able to challenge the dominant incumbent successfully. The other side of the coin is, of course, that if economies of scale in the purchase of access services are so large as to be determinative of competitive success or failure, society will be paying a high price for the continued protection of competitors from the consequences of the small scale of their operations and for preserving competitors in provision of a service that, in these circumstances, would really be a natural monopoly. The general preference of economists would be ultimately to leave determination of whether an industry is a natural monopoly to the market process itself, unimpeded by preferences such as these for smaller competitors.

The identical issue—whether incumbent monopolists should be permitted to enjoy the competitive advantage of access costs lower than those of their long-distance rivals because of the greater scale of their operations—arises in the case of the ILECs. See note 80, below.

D. Deregulation of the Retail Markets

The Telecommunications Act, in effect, seeks to resolve or at least to minimize this dilemma stemming from the fact that imposition of asymmetrical
obligations on ILECs is both *necessary* for and *antithetical* to efficient and
dynamic competition by installing conditions that would make all retail telephone markets close to perfectly contestable—sufficiently so as, paradoxi-
cally, to *permit elimination of all but the minimally essential asymmetries.*

Economists had long recognized that a critical determinant of the effectiveness of competition—and, at the extreme, a totally effective preventive of monopoly power—is what Professor Joe S. Bain termed some 40
years ago the "condition of entry:" the relative ease or difficulty of competitive entry.[70] What Professors William J. Baumol, John Panzar and
Robert Willig contributed, in their classic exposition of the concept of
contestability,[71] was its superiority to pure or perfect competition in the
presence of economies of scale and scope,[72] a full elucidation of its de-
terminants, and an intensified general recognition that under theoretically perfect contestability even a single incumbent supplier of any
particular product or service would possess no monopoly power at all.
There has been a good deal of criticism of the Baumol/Panzar/Willig argument in terms primarily of its applicability to the real world but to my
knowledge no one has disagreed with that theoretical proposition.

The determinant of contestability identified by its exponents that is critical, in the present context, is the extent to which entry entails the incurrence of sunk costs that would be wholly or partially irretrievable if the
entry proved unsuccessful.[73]

---

[70] *Barriers to New Competition*, Cambridge: Harvard University Press, 1956.

[71] *Contestable Markets and the Theory of Industry Structure*, San Diego: Harcourt
Brace and Jovanovich, 1982.

[72] In those circumstances, pure or perfect competition would, by driving prices down
to marginal costs, deny efficient firms the ability to recover their total costs.

[73] As they put it:

In brief, a perfectly contestable economic market is defined to be one into which

(continued...)

That proposition has had important practical effects. The deregulation of such industries as the airlines and trucking was rationalized, in very large measure, in terms of what was believed to be the high degree of contestability of their markets—the ease with which competitors could enter or invade one another's routes, largely by transferring their highly mobile equipment into and out as conditions justified. Subsequent experience has demonstrated that these markets are far from perfectly contestable: study after study of the behavior of air fares has confirmed that, while the presence of potential entrants has exerted a disciplining influence on price, potential entry has been substantially less powerful a discipline than the actual presence of competitors.[74]

(*...continued*)

    entry is completely free, *from which exit is costless*, in which entrants and incumbents compete on completely symmetric terms, and entry is not impeded by fear of retaliatory price alterations. (stress supplied) *Ibid.*, p. 349.

    It is the absence of sunk costs of entry that makes "exit...costless." I allude, in Section E., below, to the other requirements of contestability that the authors list here as they apply to the market for interLATA services.

[74] Gregory D. Call and Theodore E. Keeler, "Airline Deregulation, Fares and Market Behavior: Some Empirical Evidence," in Andrew F. Daughety, ed., *Analytical Studies in Transport Economics*, Cambridge: Cambridge University Press, 1985, pp. 221-47; Morrison and Winston, "Empirical Implications of the Contestability Hypothesis," *Journal of Law and Economics*, Vol. 30 (April 1987), pp. 53-66 and Gloria J. Hurdle, Richard L. Johnson, Andrew S. Joskow, Gregory J. Werden and Michael A. Williams, "Concentration, Potential Entry, and Performance In the Airline Industry," *Journal of Industrial Economics*, Vol. 38 (Dec. 1989), pp. 119-138. The fact remains that it was actual competitive entry, responding to the removal of regulatory restrictions, that vindicated the expectations that deregulation would release the forces of effective competition. Between 1979 and 1988, for example, American Airlines increased the number of hubs it served domestically from 50 to 103, United from 62 to 103, Delta from 57 to 98, Northwest from 26 to 83—the first two largely without, the second two in large measure with, the benefit of mergers. Secretary's Task Force on Competition in the U.S. Domestic Airline Industry, U.S. Dept. of Transportation, *Industry and Route Structure, Executive Summary*, Feb. 1990, p. 11. See also Winston and Morrison, *op. cit.*, pp. 128-32, showing even greater increases in the number of routes served. The entry of more than 20 new carriers in the mid-'90s, along with the continued geographic expansion of Southwest, exerted powerful competitive restraint on the incumbent carriers as the industry recovered from the catastrophic losses it suffered during the 1990-93 period. See U.S. Dept. of Transportation, *The Low Cost Airline Service Revolution*, April 1996. The

(*continued...*)

What has yet to be generally remarked is that in telecommunications the obligations imposed on the ILECs by the Telecommunications Act and complementary state policies have come as close as conceivable to making the provision of telephone services *at retail* perfectly contestable *and therefore regulation of the retail rates simply unnecessary*. What these provisions do, at the extreme, is to reduce the sunk costs associated with entry into retailing *close to zero*. It is necessary to distinguish the effect, in this respect, of the resale from the unbundled inputs provisions of the Act. So far as the former is concerned, if, as the FCC and state commissions all over the country have decided or are in process of deciding, any would-be competitor has the right to purchase any and all of an ILEC's present retail services at its retail prices less a discount large enough to enable equally efficient retailers to compete, then *all* of the ILECs' present retail markets are as close to perfectly contestable as conceivable. Rivals could at any time compete with them without having to sink a dollar into equipment that might not be fully retrievable if they decided to withdraw.

To be sure, that characterization may exaggerate the perfection of the consequent contestability of those markets. Presumably the challenging reseller would have to put in place some sort of interfaces to purchase services from the incumbent and make marketing contacts with customers and arrangements for billing them, incurring some costs that would be irretrievable upon its withdrawal from the market. (The notion of a competitive entrant having to be spared even the costs of contacting potential customers and billing them would reduce the concept of contestability to an absurdity.) But billing could always be purchased as needed and, therefore, involve no sunk cost. Resellers could also contract out for marketing as well, under terms that, similarly, would make

---

(*...continued*)

sharp increases in unrestricted fares since that time and the weakening condition or demise of many of these recent entrants have, properly, set off intense reconsiderations by government agencies of the continuing obstacles to entry, including the possibility that some of the responses to such new competition by incumbents may have been predatory.

those costs avoidable. And for AT&T or MCI, already covering virtually the entire interLATA market, those incremental costs of adding such consumer contacts for purposes of selling intraLATA and local services as well—adding some lines to their advertisements and bills—must come as close to zero as can be conceived in the real world. As the entry and continued existence of some 500 resellers of long distance services attest, these barriers to entry and exit must be close to minimal.

The requirements of the Act with respect to unbundled network elements are less likely to have such a dramatic effect *at the wholesale level*, at least initially. Certainly, if challengers are to have the ability to purchase from ILECs all the inputs necessary to duplicate the latter's offerings, without having to make any investments of their own, that is likely to make the supplying of those services at wholesale likewise highly contestable. On the other hand, presumably the challengers would have to make some financial commitment, if they chose to lease network elements from the incumbents. The ILECs would probably therefore continue, at least for a time, to enjoy monopoly power at the wholesale level.

The implications of this new situation are, nevertheless, dramatic. What it means, specifically, is that the typical requirements in governing statutes or regulations for reclassifying the entire range of *retail* local telephone services as competitive *will*, as a matter of economics, *be satisfied by these rules*.[75] In these circumstances, deregulation of the retail

---

[75] As I have already suggested, the characterization of these markets as close to perfectly contestable applies most unqualifiedly to the *performance of the retailing function*, because of the sales for resale obligations of the incumbents. If, as I have suggested, a competitor seeking instead to produce the services itself by assembly of inputs from the ILECs would incur a greater volume of sunk costs, simple deregulation of the retail markets would expose consumers to possible exploitation, as the incumbent companies raised their retail prices to which the prescribed wholesale discounts would apply. The residual protection of consumers that these considerations suggest could be ensured, however, by a continuing obligation of the *wholesaling* ILEC to make its *pre-existing* (a qualification that I will explain presently) retail services available at the prices it charged at the time of transition, less the prescribed discount—an obligation explicitly accepted by the Southern New England Telephone Company, whose reorganization proposals I proceed to describe.

operations of the ILECs becomes not just possible but mandatory. Effective competition demands that they have the identical freedom to compete at that level as is now enjoyed by their competitors, subject—with one major exception—to no obligations, handicaps or regulatory responsibilities that are not also borne by those challengers.

Before elucidating that major exception, I re-emphasize, the ILECs would under the Act, and should, remain subject to unique obligations to provide unbundled network elements and retail services at retail prices less prescribed wholesale discounts. But those *unique obligations and responsibilities are properly imposed on their wholesale components* and, for reasons I will expound presently, confined to pre-existing network elements and retail services—the locus of the presumed monopoly power that requires such regulatory offsets. It would distort competition and anti-competitively handicap the incumbents if their *retail* operations were to be subjected to asymmetrical constraints and obligations to competitors, for reasons I—and, as I have already pointed out, AT&T—have already articulated.

The most forthright proclamation of these propositions to date, to my knowledge, has been the approval by the Connecticut Department of Public Utilities Control, on June 25, 1997, of a proposal by SNET for full structural separation of a proposed wholesale and a retail subsidiary, under which the former would be subject to all the competition-protecting provisions of the Telecommunications Act and the corresponding Connecticut statutes and the latter totally free of any and all such asymmetrical burdens or obligations:

> the Department has repeatedly expressed an unwillingness to adopt any policy, position or interpretation that constitutes asymmetrical regulation in order to stimulate broader corporate participation in the telecommunications markets .... The Department will not pursue policies that simply serve to sustain an unwarranted advantage by one prospective competitor over another.[76]

---

[76] *DPUC Investigation of the Southern New England Telephone Company Affiliate Matters etc.*, Docket No. 94-10-05, *Decision*, June 25, 1997, p. 53.

This distinction that I have urged between the retail operations of the ILECs, which would be deregulated, and their wholesale operations, which would be subject to the various obligations prescribed by the Telecommunications Act, leaves unanswered the questions of what obligations, if any, would apply to the companies to make *retail* services available to their competitors at prescribed wholesale discounts. Under a proper conception of effective competition, the general rule, I believe, is that new services should not be subject to regulation—or, in the present context, to any obligations that they be shared with competitors. As Professor Joseph A. Schumpeter eloquently contended years ago, the conception of monopoly in the offer of truly new services is a virtual oxymoron. New services offer customers additional alternatives not available to them previously. Their introduction is fundamentally a competitive rather than a monopolistic phenomenon, even though they may be distinctive and the innovator may be in a position to earn supernormal profits from them. Innovation—which Schumpeter characterized graphically as a "process of creative destruction"—is a profoundly competitive phenomenon that both creates new, temporary monopolies and destroys pre-existing ones. Those temporary monopolies—such as are conferred, for example, by patents—provide both the necessary incentive and reward for risk-taking innovation, the primary key to economic progress. To deny an innovator the rewards of being first would inhibit innovation,[77] and it should not matter for these purposes whether the innovator is an incumbent telephone company or a new entrant. The Schumpeterian logic, in the present context, recommends that the ILECs be subject to the resale obligation with respect only to their present retail offerings. To impose on them any obligation to make *future* retail offerings available to competitors at the prescribed wholesale discount *and/or any innovative network elements that they develop henceforward* would be *anti-*, not pro-competitive.[78]

Given those protections and the requirement that ILECs deal at wholesale with all communications company customers, including their own retail

---

[77] *Capitalism, Socialism and Democracy*, 3rd ed., New York: Harper & Row, 1976, Chapter VII.

[78] As always, I am constrained to recognize the theoretical validity of the "infant company" qualification, such as might in the proper circumstances justify asymmetrical restraints and obligations on incumbents—subject to the many conditions and qualifications I have already spelled out.

operations, on an equal basis, there remains only one difference between the situation of the latter operations and that of the competitors (CLECs) that justifies one unique constraint on the former. The difference is, of course, the continued financial affiliation between an ILEC's wholesale and retail operations. This means that, in contrast with the situation of all the others, whatever the incumbent company "charges" its retail operations for its services—though available on the same nominal terms to all the others—goes, in effect, from one of its pockets to another. This gives rise to a possible incentive of the retailing entity or affiliate, in consideration of the overall interests of the ILEC, to be guided in its own pricing decisions not by the nominal wholesale prices it "pays" for those services but by the presumably lower marginal costs incurred by the affiliate in providing them. That incentive would motivate it to be a more vigorous competitor, to the benefit of consumers, but it also raises the familiar specter of a possible anti-competitive squeeze on its rivals at retail.

The sufficient remedy and preventive is the, by now wholly familiar, efficient component pricing rule (ECPR), which I have characterized as the rules of competitive parity[79]—and is, in fact, required by the Telecommunications Act (Sec. 272(e)(3)) insofar as carrier access charges are concerned—namely, that the ILEC be required to set its retail charges at levels sufficient to recover the same wholesale charges as it imposes on its competitors plus its own incremental costs of retailing. This is precisely the standard typically applied under the antitrust laws and embodied also in the sales for resale provisions of the Act.[80]

---

[79] For a recent restatement of the rule by its two original expositors and references and responses to critics, see William J. Baumol, Janucz A. Ordover and Robert D Willig, "Parity Pricing and Its Critics: A Necessary Condition for Efficiency in the Provision of Bottleneck Services to Competitors," *Yale Journal on Regulation*, Vol. 14, pp. 145-163 (1997); also Baumol and J. Gregory Sidak, "The Pricing of Inputs Sold to Competitors," *ibid.*, Vol. 11, pp. 172-201 (1994); the comment on that article by Kahn and Taylor, *ibid.*, pp. 225-40, and the Baumol and Sidak Rejoinder (essentially to other comments), *ibid.*, Vol. 12, pp. 177-86 (1995).

[80] Actually, the rule and the static productive efficiency it is intended to ensure require that the ILEC's retail prices recover not necessarily the *same* access fee as it charges its rivals but the same *markup* (or contribution) above incremental costs incorporated in that charge plus its incremental costs of providing access services to its own

(*continued...*)

E. Removal of the Line-of-business Restraints on the BOCs[81]

The intention of the Telecommunications Act symmetrically to lift the prohibition of the BOCs offering interLATA services within their own regions and to require them, as a condition of their liberation from that restraint, to establish the conditions I have just described for dissolution of their local monopolies (and prevent their use to exclude or handicap

---

(*...continued*)

downstream operations. This means that if its costs of providing access to itself were lower or higher than of providing that service to competitors, it would be free (in the event they were lower) or required (in the event they were higher) to reflect that difference in its own minimum permissible retail prices. See Kahn and Taylor, *op. cit.*, p. 228 and esp. note 4. Evidently because of the considerations described in note 69, above—namely, that this would permit the ILECs to charge lower toll rates than most of their competitors because the lesser volume of the latter's transactions would require them to take access at the tandem switch rather than the end office— the Telecommunications Act requires the BOCs instead simply to impute to their own retail operations access charges no lower than the amount they charge unaffiliated interexchange carriers. Sec. 272(e)(3).

While I support application of the rule to the access charges by the ILECs and their charges for essential network facilities (more precisely, the relationship between those charges and their retail prices), I have already questioned its propriety—indeed, its compatibility with effective competition—as applied to mandatory sales by the ILECs to resellers at regulatorily-prescribed discounts. See Sec. II C, above. The new Canadian deregulatory policy calls for mandatory sales for resale but only at the retail tariffs, just as in the resale requirements that the FCC imposed on AT&T (see note 67, above). Willie Grieve and Stanford L. Levin, "Telecom Competition in Canada and U.S.: The Tortoise and the Hare," *Selected Papers from The 25th Annual Telecommunications Policy Research Conference*, Alexandria, VA, Sept. 27-29, 1997, forthcoming, p. 23. Grieve and Levin cite this difference between U.S. and Canadian policy, as well as Canada's limitation of the obligation with respect to unbundled network elements to truly essential facilities (while limiting mandatory access to unbundled elements that are not essential facilities to a five-year period) as creating much greater likelihood of facilities-based competition emerging in Canada than in this country. *Ibid.*, pp. 19-20, 23 and *passim*.

[81] This discussion draws upon my experience, first as consultant with the Antitrust Division of the Department of Justice on conditions to be attached to its approval of the application of Ameritech for waivers of the interLATA restrictions in the AT&T MJF and my subsequent testimony (with Timothy J. Tardiff) in support of the application of Southwestern Bell to be permitted to offer in-region interLATA services in Oklahoma.

competitors dependent on them) is both unequivocal and unexceptionable from the standpoint of opening these markets to competition. What remain subject to intense disputation, as the RBOCs attempt to persuade the FCC for permission actually to offer the services by demonstrating that they have satisfied the statutory prerequisites, are:

- to what extent satisfaction of the law's sensible requirement that the applicant demonstrate it has indeed established the *prescribed conditions* for local competition—sensible because no one can be certain where, in what ways, and to what extent *actual* competition will prove to be economic—should require demonstration that competition has actually emerged (and, if so, how its sufficiency is to be demonstrated);

- the relative weight to be given, in assessing the public interest (as the Act requires, Sec. 271 (d) (3) (C))to the benefits of early entry by the RBOCs into the interLATA market, on the one side, and of withholding that carrot, in order to encourage their continuing cooperation in demonstrably opening their local markets to competition and refraining from discriminating against their aspiring competitors;[82]

- the extent to which the requisite demonstration should be satisfied by mere resale rather than facilities-based local competition; and, in a sense the ultimate issue,

- the efficacy of statutory and regulatory (and antitrust) safeguards against the BOCs' abusing their residual monopoly power at the local level to unfairly disadvantage their interLATA competitors, once they have actually been awarded permission to compete with them. These include accounting safeguards, cost allocations and

---

[82] See the measured advocacy of the latter course by Professor Marius Schwartz in his affidavit of May 14, 1997, prepared for the Antitrust Division of the Department of Justice—a "modest delay" in granting Southwestern Bell's request for permission to offer in-region interLATA services and requiring the actual presence of competition (of unspecified dimensions) as the index of whether the local exchange markets have been irrevocably opened, but permitting the RBOCs to rebut the presumption that their actions were responsible in situations in which competitive entry had not occurred.

rules governing transactions among affiliates developed and administered by regulators over many years to preclude anti-competitive cross-subsidizations and the fully-separated sub-sidiary requirements for the competitive operations prescribed by the Telecommunications Act.

Unsurprisingly, the same kinds of issues are beginning to be contested hotly in the electric industry, particularly as several states have been moving to open it to competition at the retail level:

- What, if any, are the public benefits of continued financial integration between generation, which is generally believed to be potentially competitive, and transmission and local distribution, which have proved to be naturally monopolistic?

- What is the case for and against the local distribution company performing the two functions that have hitherto not been clearly distinguished—local transport, which is apparently naturally monopolistic, and the competitive merchandising of energy services—aggregating and selling the power along with ancillary services. Also, in which category do metering, billing, hook-ups and disconnections belong?

- To the extent the monopolistic and potentially competitive functions are conducted by financially affiliated entities, how effective will regulatory constraints, codes of conduct and prescriptions of equal access be in assuring equal competitive opportunities to non-affiliated rival generators and marketers?[83]

---

[83] Some of the most challenging demands for separation of utility and non-utility operations of the incumbent electric and gas companies and for the most detailed prohibitions of their exerting assertedly unfair competitive advantages have been coming from the ENRON Capital & Trade Resources Corp. See, e.g. its petition to the California Public Utilities Commission for an Order Instituting Rule Making on Standards of Conduct for Marketing Affiliates, Dec. 3, 1996; its comments before the Pennsylvania Public Utility Commission's Competitive Safeguards Working Group, April 25, 1997; and its sponsored direct testimony by Michael Dirmeier and Malcolm Jacobson in the latter proceeding, July 2, 1997, Docket No. R-00973954, Re: PP&L restructuring—Surrebuttal, Aug. 15, 1997.

As this listing of general issues clearly suggests—especially in consideration of the enormous stakes involved—these controversies in the telephone industry have been both intense and extremely wide-ranging, raising such issues as:

- the sufficiency of competition in interLATA markets currently, without benefit of participation by the RBOCs; in particular the extent to which its benefits have extended to small residential users;[84]

- how much of a difference RBOC entry would make;

- the relative detectability of discriminations by the BOCs in the quality of access or interconnection services provided, respectively, to their own downstream affiliates and to their rivals— discriminations that would have to be sufficiently perceptible to consumers to induce them either to shun or discontinue subscription to those competitive services yet not perceptible enough to be recorded in the quality-of-service monitorings by both regulatory commissions and such competitor-customers as the major long-distance carriers;

- the weight and interpretation to be given to the actual experience of apparently successful competition between the vertically integrated RBOCs and rivals requiring access to their facilities for the provision of cellular, paging and voice messaging services; customer-premises equipment; intraLATA toll; interLATA toll in the major corridor markets, notably between New York and New Jersey, to which the interLATA proscription has not applied; interLATA offerings by ILECs other than the BOCs, such as GTE, United, Rochester Telephone and, since 1994, SNET, to which the proscription has not or no longer applies;

- the weight to be placed on the numerous complaints of assertedly anti-competitive tactics and resistances by the RBOCs to specific demands by competitors for collocations of facilities, access to network elements or retail services for resale.

---

[84] See reference to the 1991-97 experience at note 187, below.

It would extend this paper grotesquely to attempt to summarize the competing arguments and proffers of evidence on these many subjects; it might also be regarded as inappropriate, in view of my own participation in these controversies on behalf of RBOCs. In these circumstances, I offer only the following observations from one of those participations that establish the connection between the proceedings to date on the interLATA proscription and one central thesis of this article—namely, the inherent tendency of regulators to go beyond merely opening markets to competition and micromanage the actual entry and survival of competitors:

> There has accumulated, over the last decade or more, a great deal of actual experience with competition between the RBOCs—and LECs that are not BOCs—on the one side, and rivals dependent on access to their facilities. An ounce of actual experience is surely weightier than a pound of speculation about possible misdeeds or, indeed, of anecdotal claims about exclusionary practices. Assertions about the theoretical inadequacies of regulatory safeguards against predation, cross-subsidy and discriminatory treatment of competitors simply ignore this historical evidence. In practice, competition by non-vertically integrated firms with RBOC 'bottleneck monopolies' has already succeeded in other telecommunications markets that are at least as susceptible to anti-competitive tactics as the interLATA market ...

> Professors Hubbard and Lehr, Hall and Shapiro collectively provide a laundry list of complaints of assertedly anticompetitive tactics by RBOCs, evidently under the assumption that where there is smoke there must be fire. Neither we nor they are in a position to evaluate each of these complaints. But differences of opinion, conflicts of interest and complaints are inevitable in negotiations of the kinds of arrangements between the ILECs and their competitors contemplated by the Act and necessary if there is to be efficient and effective competition.

> It was precisely in recognition of the inevitability of such disagreements that Congress provided a procedure for the negotiations that it recognized would be necessary, for arbitration of differences and resolution by regulatory commissions, all under

a tight time schedule. And the process is unquestionably work-ing: to date, in Oklahoma alone, 48 companies have requested negotiations with SWBT and 19 of these companies (including Sprint) have successfully concluded negotiations without re-quests for mediation and without the need for arbitration. Of all the companies negotiating with SWBT in Oklahoma, AT&T has been the only one that has required the OCC to intervene through arbitration. This is a truly remarkable record of achievement.[85]

The FCC turned down the Southwestern Bell application for Oklahoma and, more recently, that of Ameritech for Michigan,[86] in both cases on the similar recommendation of the Department of Justice, on the ground that the companies had not, in fact, met the statutory requirements[87] with respect to either the actual presence of local competition or their having

---

[85] Reply Affidavit of Alfred E. Kahn and Timothy J. Tardiff before the FCC, *In the Matter of Application of SBC Communications, Inc., et al, for Provision of In-Region, InterLATA Services in Oklahoma*, May 27, 1997 (pars. 50 and 51). I cannot re-frain from the self-indulgence of alluding to AT&T's assertion, in another proceeding, that the deregulation of its retailing operations, in contrast with its wholesale operations, requested by SNET should await the entry of *facilities-based* competition at the local level. In view of AT&T's apparent policy of ubiquitously demanding the right to *purchase* retail services from ILECs at commission-pre-scribed discounts, and its consistent advocacy of regulatorily-prescribed discounts so generous and LEC charges for use of their own facilities so low as actively to dis-courage competitors from constructing their own facilities—as I will document more fully in part III, below—I have observed that the AT&T witness must have had Joseph Heller, author of *Catch 22*, as a silent collaborator. For a similar accusation directed against the FCC itself, see Thomas J. Duesterberg and Kenneth Gordon, *Competition and Deregulation in Telecommunications, The Case for a New Para-digm*, Indianapolis: Hudson Institute, 1997, pp. 77-83.

[86] *Application of Ameritech Michigan Pursuant to Section 271 of the Telecommunica-tions Act of 1996 to Provide In-Region, InterLATA service in Michigan*, CC Docket No. 97-137, filed May 21, 1997.

[87] *In the Oklahoma case*, the Commission found there was not actually in being a lo-cal competitor serving both business and residential customers and that the RBOC did not qualify for the alternative statutory treatment ("Track B") of demonstrating its satisfaction of the checklist of required enabling actions on the ground that that alternative was to have been available only to BOCs that had not received any bona fide application for interconnection. *Memorandum Opinion and Order*, CC Docket No. 97-121, Adopted June 25, 1997, pars. 13-22.

fulfilled all their stipulated responsibilities for making it possible. The ultimately relevant point here is, however, that whatever one's judgment of the merits of the FCC's reading of the law in these two cases, these decisions may, nevertheless, reasonably be cited as continuing manifestations of the policy of micromanaging the entry and survival of competitors that this paper seeks to document.

It seems to me they clearly may be so described, for a number of reasons. As Tardiff and I pointed out, the Act prescribes a *procedure* for *opening* local markets to competition, as a condition for lifting the ban on inter-LATA offering by the BOCs—a procedure for negotiations between them and applicants for access, interconnection or purchases for resale; arbitration, if requested by either party; and agreements approved by state commissions, all within 10 months of the first request for negotiations. As of late November 1997, some 1,700 agreements had been completed under that process, according to the tally of the U.S. Telephone Association, and the state commissions have both the authority and responsibility to see to it that the ILECs comply with those undertakings in good faith. What the FCC and Department of Justice have clearly presumed to do is go beyond superintending that process and judge the *sufficiency* of resulting competition. As I have already pointed out, the Department endorsed the recommendation of Professor Marius Schwartz to this effect, which effectively added an essentially regulatory process to the one prescribed in the law. First, the commission would be obliged to satisfy itself that the amount of competition that actually emerged was sufficient, and, second, the RBOCs would have the opportunity—indeed, would be obliged—to rebut the presumption that any insufficiency of competition that the Commission may have found was *their fault*.

The aptness of this characterization is further underlined by the consideration that in at least one of the markets affected, the interLATA, it is inconceivable that granting the applications could have any effect on *competition* other than to invigorate it. As Timothy Tardiff and I argued, in conclusion:

> The ultimate economic question is whether SBC and the other BOCs can possibly, by the exercise of such diminishing but residual monopoly power at the local level as they possess, succeed in suppressing competition as an effective force in the market they wish

to enter—suppress <u>competition</u>, that is to say, as contrasted with discommoding <u>competitors</u>.

And this leads to our final and in a real sense definitive point. We find the ultimate essential component of the successful strategy of cross-subsidization, predation or exclusionary tactics hypothesized by opponents of BOC entry into the interLATA market—namely, the permanent removal or disabling of competitors sufficient to enable the predator to recover the costs of those cross-subsidizations or other schemes by <u>raising prices</u>—flatly inconceivable. The incumbent long-distance providers are in command of 100 percent of the market. They have installed capacity that is not going to go away. The marginal cost of operating it is low, leaving its owners with latitude for matching price reductions more than sufficient to dissuade any would-be predator. It is the present long-distance companies that are the dominant firms in that market. In these circumstances, we find it simply inconceivable that they would or could either be driven out of business or be so debilitated by discriminatory tactics practiced by the BOCs as to weaken the protection of their continued competitive presence. In these circumstances, entry by SBC and the other RBOCs could only be beneficial <u>to consumers</u>.[88]

These last considerations pass over the fact that the Act seeks to encourage competition at the *local* level *for its own sake* and not merely to ensure fair competition in the interLATA market. It seeks to do so, however, by requiring the ILECs to *make available* to rivals the stipulated required tools. We agree with *that* requirement; it is Professor Schwartz's proposal of an additional hurdle that we reject.[89]

This strategy of the Justice Department and evidently of the FCC of withholding permission to enter the interLATA market in order to maintain

---

[88] Affidavit *In the Matter of Application of SBC Communications Inc.*, op. cit., Feb. 13, 1997, pars. 74-75.

[89] Reply Affidavit in the same proceeding, *op. cit.*, par 68.

greater pressure on the BOCs to accommodate local competitors evidently fails to weigh in the balance a corollary of that proposition—namely, the powerful incentive that their approach imparts to the long-distance carriers to make unreasonable demands on the ILECs, complaining about their asserted failure to bargain with them in good faith, *in order* to forestall their competition in the interLATA business. Moreover, any such interpretation of the Act raises another opposing consideration—which Professor Schwartz also mentions[90] but evidently fails to weigh in the balance—on the side of promptly lifting that prohibition: namely, the important contribution it would make toward the intensification of long-distance competition *intra*LATA: Under the Act, the extension of presubscription for intraLATA service from Dec. 19, 1995, onward is made contingent on and simultaneous with permitting the BOCs to compete interLATA. Since basic local rates to most subscribers are already repressed below efficient levels, whereas intraLATA toll rates remain egregiously inflated, it seems clear that the direct benefits of the introduction of presubscription to competitive IXCs for the latter services offers a far greater potential for consumer benefit than such incremental encouragement to competition in the provision of local services as retaining the ban would impart. This consideration is even more compelling in view of the fact that the resale provisions of the Act already offer CLECs a ready opportunity, by purchasing the subsidized services from the incumbent LECs, to bring the benefits of competition to the provision of such *over*priced local services as Custom Calling features.

---

[90] Schwartz, p. 30.

III. Deregulating Deregulation—
or, Resisting the High Marginal Propensity to Micromanage

The continued responsibility of public utility regulatory commissions to ensure access by challengers to essential network facilities at reasonable rates presents them with a temptation—indeed, in a sense, a responsibility—to micromanage the process of deregulation itself. They have no choice but to set ceilings on those wholesale prices, along with the other terms on which the incumbent firms are to be required to make their facilities and retail services available to their challengers.

At the same time, there is every difference between regulatory interventions establishing the conditions under which competition may be relied on to determine the outcome and interventions intended, whether consciously or unconsciously, to *dictate* that outcome. The past several years have presented numerous illustrations of commissions succumbing to the latter temptation, deliberately or inadvertently.

A. The Continued Recourse to Cost Allocations

Since "just and reasonable" rates are supposed to be based on cost, regulators have by long-standing tradition engaged in the process of allocating the total costs of utility companies among their several services, as well as between regulated and unregulated services, to establish the basis for individual rates. Those allocations—and the prices based on them—raised important questions of economic efficiency and equity even when companies operated as franchised monopolists. Controversies over the proper treatment or apportionment of the cost of the subscriber loop go back at least to the proceedings in the 1920s that culminated in the Supreme Court's decision in *Smith v. Illinois Bell*. I have already alluded to the massive economic welfare losses that the resulting gross overcharging of long-distance usage has entailed.[91] Those same issues become additionally intense—and cost allocations an even more important form of micromanagement—in the presence of unregulated competitors and competition. For these reasons it becomes necessary, however summarily, to restate some elementary economic propositions:

1. The concept of "cost" has no meaning in either economics or logic except in terms of *causation*. When we say that drunk driving "costs" us so many lives per year or so many dollars in property damage, we can mean only that the practice *causes* us, individually and/or collectively, to suffer those consequences. Similarly, when we say that the "cost" of a subscriber loop is some amount, it can mean nothing except that some act of purchase by a consumer *causes* a telephone company and society to incur that cost. In order to set efficient prices we must then determine *which* act of purchase has that effect.

2. Consumers impose the cost of the loop on a telephone company and on society by the act of subscribing to telephone service. The causation principle therefore requires that the cost of providing the loop be fully incorporated in the cost of that basic service, that is, in a flat one-time or periodic charge. Conversely, if, as I understand to be essentially the case, actual use of the loop for local or long distance calling or for other services imposes *no* loop costs on the supplier and if subscribers were to refrain from placing those calls or using any of those other services it would not *save* any of those costs,[92] there is no sense in which usage or

---

[91] See the criticism of the "separations" authorized by *Smith v. Illinois Bell* in my *The Economics of Regulation*, Vol. 1, pp. 100, n. 39 and 152-53 and discussion of that specific decision in Kahn and Zielinski, "New Rate Structures in Communications," Part II, *Public Utilities Fortnightly,* April 8, 1976, pp. 9-11.

[92] See the discussion of contentions to the contrary—including, prominently, contentions that the *design* of the network is affected by prospective usage—in my (with William B. Shew) "Current Issues in Telecommunications Regulation: Pricing" *Yale Journal on Regulation* , Vol. 4, No. 2 (Spring 1987), pp. 191, 210-32; also David Gabel and Mark D. Kennet, "Pricing of Telecommunications Services," *Review of Industrial Organization*, Vol. 8 (1993), pp. 1-14; the comments by Lester D.

(continued...)

other services can be held causally responsible for them.[93]

It should by now be unnecessary to recount the full, dreary history of attempts by regulatory commissions and "consumer representatives" to justify allocating some of the costs of the loop to usage—preponderantly toll calling and access charges to long-distance service providers.[94]

At the same time, the persistence and ingenuity of economists—typically hired to represent the benighted staffs of some regulatory commissions—in finding new rationalizations for allocating some portion of the

---

(*...continued*)

Taylor, William E. Taylor and by me, along with their reply, *ibid.*, pp. 15-47. In general terms, the proper response is that efficient prices would reflect the marginal costs actually incurred by a supply network efficiently designed to serve the demands actually placed on it, with the costs of errors in that design imprudently incurred borne by the suppliers in the component of rates reflecting return on their sunk (i.e., non-marginal) investment costs.

[93] On the FCC's previous recognition of this principle, see note 13, above. It has now—once again—asserted its intention to phase local loop and other non-traffic-sensitive costs out of usage-sensitive interstate access charges "and direct ... incumbent local exchange carriers (LECs) to recover those NTS [non-traffic-sensitive] costs through more economically efficient, flat-rated charges." *In the Matter of Access Charge Reform etc.*, CC Docket No. 96-262 etc., *First Report and Order*, adopted May 7, 1997 (hereinafter, *Access Charge Reform Order*), pars. 6 and 17-37.

As I understand it, these generalizations do not apply to wireless telephony, where subscribers do not have dedicated access facilities and usage produces congestion. In that service it is the dedicated purchased or leased customer equipment whose costs are analogous to those of the subscriber line. For a discussion of the efficiency principle applicable to the pricing, respectively, of the instrument itself and its usage, see Section A.3, below.

[94] See the dissection of the "Six Pricing Fallacies" in Kahn and Shew, *op.cit*, pp. 200-210; also S.G. Parsons, "Seven Years After Kahn and Shew: Lingering Myths on Costs and Pricing Telephone Service," *Yale Journal on Regulation*, Vol. 11 (1994), pp. 149-70; the continued insistence by Gabel (*op. cit.*, p. 32ff) that because the subscriber loop is a "shared facility," its costs must be allocated to its several uses, and the effective response of Banerjee, *op. cit.*, pp. 29-34.

costs of the loop out of the basic residential charge[95] and the incompatibility of such arbitrary prices with efficient competition suggest it is desirable to describe and refute some of the more recent, superficially plausible rationalizations.

1. The TSLRIC quagmire

One such comparatively recent rationalization[96] builds on the increasingly prevalent practice of utility commissions basing purportedly efficient prices on the incremental costs of an entire service (TSLRIC)—the cost added by adding that service to a mix of other services or saved if the entire service were dropped. The argument proceeds from Faulhaber's definition of that cost[97]: where facilities are shared by two or more services, the incremental cost of service B is the difference between the cost of providing service A on a stand-alone basis and the cost of providing service A and B together. If, then, the telephone system is conceived of as providing three separate services—subscriber dial tone, local calling and long-distance calling—the TSLRIC of the first of these

---

[95] See my exposure of the circularity or teleological character of these exercises—

> Full cost allocations that are not grounded in causality have no basis in objective reality; they have no meaning *independent* of the prices they are supposed to justify except in some ritualistic, incantational sense .... they are merely a plausible, conventional device for justifying some preconceived notion of what the proper *prices* should be ....

in "The Uneasy Marriage of Regulation and Competition," *Telematics*, Vol. 1, No. 5, September 1984, p. 12.

> As John T. Wenders has put it:

> costs can be discovered, costs can be identified, costs can be estimated: But costs cannot be allocated. They are not a pie to be divided up among consumers.

The Economics of Telecommunications, Cambridge, MA: Ballinger Publishing Company, 1987, p. 59.

[96] Testimony of Ben Johnson, Pennsylvania Public Utility Commission, Docket No. I-940035, Dec. 19, 1995, p.17.

[97] Gerald R. Faulhaber, "Cross-Subsidization: Pricing in Public Enterprises," *The American Economic Review*, Vol. 65 (Dec. 1975), pp. 966-977.

would be close to zero if not actually zero, since any system set up to supply the other two services would already have to incorporate the loop that provides the first of them.[98] So a "theoretically pure" TSLRIC of mere subscriber dial tone (or of the loop) would be close to zero.

To this ingenious, but misguided, line of argument, there are several answers, progressively definitive:

First, to define "basic service" as not essentially equivalent to the loop is to define *Hamlet* without the Prince of Denmark. The loop is not merely an essential part of the basic telephone service that it is our national policy to make universally affordable and subscribed to; it is at the *heart* of that service—the lifeline connection between subscribers and the rest of society.[99] It is the loop attaching subscribers to the system that gives rise to the network externalities—the value to every subscriber of being able to *reach* other subscribers—which are at the heart of the economic case for directly subsidizing its provision. It is the decision of consumers to *subscribe* to telephone service, whether or not they then use it to place calls, that is causally responsible for imposing the cost of the loop on society.[100]

Second, application of TSLRIC as the measure of incremental costs produces the *identical result* when applied to the other services that use the loop: by the same reasoning, the loop portion of the separate TSLRICs of local and long-distance calling are close to zero, because it would already

---

[98] Observe that this version of the argument, frequently proffered, does not include the variation (see, e.g., Gabel and Kennet, *op. cit.*) that a system designed for subscriber access alone would differ from one designed for usage of varying volumes.

[99] This is not to deny that we might wish also to subsidize calling. It is only to insist that rational policy-making must be grounded in a recognition of the distinct differences in the respective incremental costs of the two services.

[100] I owe to Lee Selwyn the analogy between subscription to the loop and purchase of an automobile in defining the efficient pricing of each. The fact that a telephone subscriber can use the capacity provided by the loop for a variety of purposes or not at all does not change the transaction that imposes its costs on society, any more than whether an owner uses his car for local or long-distance, business or pleasure travel or not at all. Manifestly, recovering the costs of cars only from their *use*—for example, by a tax on gasoline—would inefficiently encourage purchase of costly cars and discourage driving.

have had to be installed to offer the other. TSLRIC provides no assistance therefore in determining which transactions are causally responsible for its cost and should, therefore, pay for it if economic efficiency is to be served.

The resolution of this apparent dilemma is that TSLRIC is not the sole determinant of the competitive or the minimum efficient price of any good or service. As William Baumol, the originator of that concept, has pointed out, the minimum efficient price is TSLRIC *or* the LRIC of smaller increments, *whichever is higher.*[101] The additional cost imposed on a telephone

---

[101] Baumol and Sidak, *Toward Competition in Local Telephony*, Cambridge: The MIT Press, 1994, pp. 67-68. It is unnecessary at this point to do more than record my disagreement with the authors' assertion that the correct floor is always the higher of the two; it is the LRIC of the relevant increment of output or sales that is the proper floor in situations in which it is *below* TSLRIC. The logic is both simple and compelling. TSLRIC is by its very nature an *average* cost—the average cost per unit of adding an entire service. Professor Baumol himself has been foremost among the exponents of the proposition that, where, as is ubiquitously the case in telecommunications, the added costs entailed in taking on smaller increments of business (LRIC) are lower than those average costs, economic efficiency requires that sellers be permitted to price down to that lower level in order to obtain or retain that incremental business. See also William E. Taylor, Testimony on behalf of NYNEX before the Vermont Public Service Board, Docket Nos. 5700-5702, July 5, 1994, pp. 17-21, and my own assertion,

> the proper size of the incremental unit of output [to be costed in this way] depends on the perspective of the decision under consideration ...

Following this principle, I observed,

> When the decision is one to extend or withdraw an entire service to some particular block of customers ... the relevant unit of output is clearly the entire service in question.

(In the section in my *The Economics of Regulation*, "Specifying the Incremental Block of Output," Vol. 1, pp. 76-77.)

By the same token, as William Vickrey explained,

> The increment in traffic for which the cost increment is to be estimated should have a composition similar to the increment induced by the rate change under consideration ... Thus *unless a policy is being contemplated of suppressing a class of service entirely, the traffic increment for which the cost is being ascertained should never be an entire class of traffic*, but only a final increment in that traffic corresponding to a realistically contemplated rate change. (*Ibid.*, p. 108n.,

(continued...)

company by taking on an additional subscriber or some group of subscribers in a newly settled locality is obviously not zero or anything close to zero, but includes, before anything else, the cost of the loop itself.[102]

(*...continued*)

> citing his Testimony in FCC Dockets 16258 and 15011, *In the Matter of American Telephone and Telegraph Company*, Networks Exhibit No. 5, July 22, 1968, mimeo., 23-24. Stress supplied.)

This same issue of defining the relevant increment arises also in the context of defining the grouping of products or services to which the efficient component pricing or imputation rule is to be applied. Manifestly, compliance of the incumbent carriers should be tested not against each individual competitive service or subcategory but to the collection of services subject to competition. See, e.g., my testimony on this issue, dated March 24, 1997, in the SNET reorganization proceedings (note 76, above):

> As the identity between this requirement of the imputation or efficient component pricing rule ("ECPR") and the proscription under the antitrust laws of predatory squeezes clearly suggests, application of this test calls first for an economically correct *definition of the relevant market*. Does it mean, for example, that SAI [the proposed unregulated retail subsidiary] would be required to satisfy the test for every single one of its prices of every single one of its separate services—for local calls under measured service after 6:00 p.m., for example? Or interLATA calls? The answer is *absolutely not*. SAI should be no more subject to such a restriction on each of the individual components of the packages of services that it offers customers than its rivals—than AT&T is or should be, for example, with respect to its 5 cents a minute charge for intraLATA toll service in Connecticut, a price that could clearly not, considered separately, satisfy ECPR, since the access charges it pays to an ILEC like SNET for such calls, at originating and termination ends, alone add up to about five cents a minute.

> The "relevant market"—to which the ECPR, identically with the antitrust proscription of anti-competitive squeezes, would apply—must embrace the entire range of services in the sale of which SAI and its rivals compete or could readily compete. For example, interexchange carriers offer residential and business customers a complete package of toll calling service, over various distances and times of day. Accordingly, the SAI retail charge or charges to assess would be its entire schedule of toll charges for the group of services to particular customer groups for whose patronage it is competing. That is the price that competitors for that business have to meet; the relevant question is whether SAI makes money in providing that package to that group of customers, after meeting the imputation requirement.

[102] Failure to include that cost in the charge for subscription will tend to encourage wasteful over-subscription. Much more serious from the standpoint of economic efficiency—since the demand for subscription to telephone service is highly

(*continued...*)

2. The joint products fallacy

A good deal of the ancient controversy has hinged on the question of whether the costs of the loop are properly regarded as the costs of providing *joint* products such as local and long-distance calling and, perhaps separately, dialtone, or whether they are properly defined as *common* products. The critical distinction is that joint products—strictly defined as products economically producible only in fixed, invariable proportions—do not have separate marginal *production* costs, whereas products produced in *common* do have such costs, which can be ascertained by increasing or decreasing the output of one of them while holding the others constant. In response to the consideration that subscribers do indeed "consume" the various telephone services in varying proportions, so that those services are clearly not joint products, Ben Johnson has recently offered the refinement that the loop itself does at one and the same time provide a fixed, joint

> *capacity* available for placing and receiving all three types of calls[:] the telephone company cannot increase the capacity for local calls without concurrently increasing the capacity for toll calls. In this sense, it clearly fits within the definition of joint costs ...[103]

The answer to this contention—even if we accept Johnson's characterization of the capacity provided by the loop as "jointly" available for several services—is that while joint products do not have separate marginal *production* or *supply* costs, they nevertheless have differing marginal *opportunity* costs and, correspondingly, efficient prices.[104] A natural gas

---

(*...continued*)

inelastic—is that the transfer of the burden of recovering those costs to the charges for usage discourages use of the system the cost of which to society would be lower than the benefit to subscribers. (On the implications of the probably higher elasticity of demand for second than for first lines, see Section VI.B.)

[103]   *Op. cit.* Appendix B, p.11, Stress supplied. This rationalization is identical to Gabel's, based on identifying the loop as a "shared facility" or "input." See note 94, above.

[104] See my *The Economics of Regulation*, Vol. 1, pp. 77-83, drawing on Jack Hirshleifer, "Peak Loads and Efficient Pricing: Comment," *Quarterly Journal of Economics* (August 1958), Vol. 72, pp. 458-459.

pipeline, similarly, provides capacity to carry gas "jointly" in summer and winter, a carpentry shop "jointly" to produce lumber and sawdust. The relevant economic question is what is added to society's costs if consumers purchase somewhat more, and what costs would society save if they purchased somewhat less, of the *products* for which that capacity is an input. If indeed the costs of the loop do not vary depending upon the number of local or toll calls placed on it, then incorporating some portion of those costs in the prices for those uses of it, by exaggerating their incremental or avoidable costs, inefficiently discourages that usage. For those uses, therefore, the loop is a pure byproduct, a free good, just like pipeline carriage of gas in the summer or sawdust in a carpentry shop, and it inefficiently discourages those uses to recover in their price any portion of the costs of the "joint capacity"—or, in Gabel's terminology, "shared input"—that makes them possible.

3. The offsetting contribution from complementary services

A third manifestation of the continuing incentive of economists to respond to the demand, especially by commission staffs, for ever more ingenious rationalizations of allocating some of the costs of the loop to usage is the contention that residential service recovers all of its incremental costs "on a total service basis." As one witness has put it,

> the local loop is analogous to a 'kiosk' which allows a service provider to see [sell] a variety of services ... Requiring that the entire 'kiosk' (the local loop) be recovered solely from local exchange service would introduce distortions in a competitive local exchange market.[105]

The simple answer is that it is tautological to reduce the calculated incremental cost of basic service by crediting against it the net revenues from other, overpriced complementary services, thereby "justifying" its

---

[105] Testimony of Trevor Roycroft, Before the Public Service Commission of Maryland, *In the Matter of the Inquiry into Alternative Forms of Regulating Telephone Companies,* Case No. 8715, Feb. 15, 1996, pp. 17, 19-20.

underpricing. This logic uses the overpricing of usage services, relative to their incremental costs (both TS and for smaller increments), to justify the underpricing of basic service—assertedly on a cost basis. It uses the *proceeds* from the cross subsidy to prove there is no subsidy.[106] Instead of independently establishing the respective incremental costs of these services on a causal basis in order then to calculate efficient prices, it translates the present inefficient prices into fraudulent measures of cost, in a totally circular and self-justifying fashion.[107]

But, the ever resourceful defenders of the present rate structure protest, firms in competitive industries frequently offer pure access free or below cost, choosing to take their profits instead from the sale of services to which it gives customers access.[108] Familiar examples are the free parking at suburban parking malls or the offer of distinctively styled razors below cost in the expectation of selling above cost razor blades especially designed to fit them. A more recent example is the way in which cellular phone companies have been competing for subscribers by offering them the requisite equipment at very low prices. Gabel and Kennet cite the practice of some credit card companies not charging annual fees,

---

[106] The inquiry it calls for *is* relevant to the question: Are *residential customers* collectively being subsidized? It is irrelevant to the question: Is *basic residential service* efficiently priced?

[107] As I will observe at a later point, this "costing" procedure, and the continued under-pricing of basic residential service that it seeks to justify, has the additional defect of being progressively incompatible with the competition that has been permeating these markets and that it is our national policy to encourage—which in turn explains the perceived need to find alternative, competitively-neutral sources of subsidy. I have commented at greater length on this tautological argument in "Pricing of Telecommunications Services: A Comment," *Review of Industrial Organization*, Vol. 8 (1993), p. 41, note 5.

[108] Sometimes these assertions take the more extreme form that sellers in competitive industries "never" charge for the mere option to use their facilities or to purchase other services to which it provides them access. As William Shew and I have pointed out, that statement is patently incorrect. Hotels recover their costs primarily in charges for mere "access" to the rooms; providers of commercial and residential properties charge rent for access to office or housing space, whether "used" or not; golf and tennis clubs charge membership fees; credit card issuers, flat service charges per month or year. *Op. cit.*, pp. 202-204.

despite the undeniable fixed, non-usage-sensitive costs of mere subscription to the service.[109]

Since William Shew and I have elsewhere rebutted these proffered justifications of underpricing residential subscriber access to the telephone
network— "mere" dial tone—I list the principal responses only briefly.
Whether competitive markets offer these kinds of access free, or below
cost, depends on

- the dimensions of the respective incremental costs of access and
  usage relative to

- the costs of administering separate charges for each;

- the possibilities of free ridership and consequent incurrence of
  opportunity costs if access is not charged for separately; and

- the relative elasticities and cross elasticities of the demands for
  the complementary services—in particular, the responsiveness of
  the demand for usage to the price of access.

For example, the cost of providing parking spaces at suburban malls—as
contrasted with the cost of providing hotel rooms, residential and commercial real-estate, golf courses or telephone dial-tone—is only a small
fraction of the total cost of providing the goods and services sold at those
malls. In addition, the danger of "free parkers" using the space for purposes other than shopping there and crowding out local shoppers is negligible, as contrasted with parking lots and garages in center cities,
which, therefore, do charge full cost. Competition in unregulated markets
often involves—indeed introduces—a great deal of price discrimination
in favor of demand-elastic or low "value of service" customers: witness
the positive association of such discrimination with airline competition.[110] The elasticity of demand for *subscription* to cellular telephone

---

[109] *Op. cit.*, "Reply to Comments," *Review of Industrial Organization*, Vol. 8 (1993), p. 44.

[110] Severin Borenstein and Nancy L. Rose, "Competition and Price Dispersion in the
U.S. Airline Industry," Working Paper No. 3785, Cambridge: National Bureau of
Economic Research, July 1991.

service is probably higher than for usage of the service, once subscribed to, and undoubtedly far higher than for basic telephone service. Similarly, potential users of credit cards may be more sensitive to the fixed fee than the careless or more profligate among them to the interest charge on unpaid balances. So here competition has produced a combination of give-away cellular equipment with high-markup cellular usage; give-away credit card service with high interest charges: that is where the big money is. In these cases, selling underpriced cellular phones, credit cards (and razors) and overpriced cellular usage, credit (and razor blades) is an effective means of price discrimination. The latter serve as counting devices to identify users for whom the value of the combined service is high and charge them correspondingly more, in the aggregate, than customers for whom the consumer surplus is relatively low, as reflected in their relatively few purchases of razor blades, cellular usage or credit.

In situations in which prices uniformly set at marginal costs would not recover total costs, such price discriminations can clearly be welfare-enhancing. I suspect this is the case with cellular phone service, airlines and probably also goods sold in shopping malls. It would certainly not make economic sense to prohibit it in unregulated industries generally.

Nor should it be forsworn in regulated industries, either, for exactly the same reason. But that fact does not exempt its specific applications from the necessity of complying with the relevant principles I have just summarized. The justifications I have inferred in the several examples just described clearly do not apply to or justify the underpricing of residential dial tone, the incremental costs of which are very high and the demand highly inelastic relative to those of usage.[111]

---

[111] As I have already suggested, where, as in most of these examples, first-best, marginal cost pricing is not feasible and some of the products or services are complementary, it is necessary, in designing second-best efficient prices, to take into account the cross-elasticities of their demands. The demand for the goods sold in shopping malls, credit card loans, and for cellular telephone service might well be more responsive to the price of admission—parking in the first case, the fixed fee in the second, the cost of the equipment in the third—than to the "usage" charges themselves. In that event, the price discrimination (or "counting") effected by pricing the

(continued...)

B. Allocating the Costs of Joint Facilities and Operations Between Regulated and Unregulated Services

In documenting the tendency of regulatory commissions to handicap utility companies in their competitive exploitation of economies of scale and scope, in order to ensure the emergence or survival of competitors, we have recognized the convergence of that goal with the desire to hold down the price of utility services—and to receive political credit for doing so. The efficient and equitable distribution of the benefits of these economies is of course a legitimate function of regulation; unfortunately, it also affords ample opportunities for protectionism and kleptocratic behavior.

One such prominent occasion is the apparent need to apportion the costs of rapidly expanding facilities capable of supplying both regulated and unregulated services—of which fiberoptic cable for carrying telephone and video signals is the outstanding example. Since regulators are under instructions to base their regulated rates on "cost," it would seem they are obliged to determine what portion of the costs of these common facilities is properly recovered in the regulated rates or—the other side of the coin—to shelter purchasers of utility services from costs properly attributable to the unregulated operations. These exercises are frequently rationalized additionally by the consideration that to the extent the utility companies are enabled to reap profits from the unregulated ventures because of capabilities—facilities, managerial talents, the products of research developed and paid for by purchasers of the regulated services, or customer good will stemming from their franchised monopolies—purchasers of the regulated services are entitled to some reimbursement or sharing in those profits.

(*...continued*)

former services at zero and below marginal costs, respectively, and the complementary products or services correspondingly above marginal costs is probably welfare-enhancing. But it is almost certainly not true that telephone usage is more sensitive to the admission fee—the charge for dialtone alone—than to its own direct charges—so the logic of the practice in unregulated industries frequently cited by defenders of the regulated telephone rate structures simply does not apply. See Kahn and Shew, *op. cit.*, pp. 251-252.

Some of these contentions are either demagogic or ignorant. For example, they sometimes take the form of an argument that to the extent these ventures are financed out of undistributed profits or depreciation recoveries of the utility companies, they were really "paid for" and "belong" to the monopoly ratepayers. The simple answer is that ratepayers paid those costs of the services they received when they received them. The depreciation and profit components of the prices they paid represented reimbursements to the companies of economic costs already incurred in providing service and clearly belong to them to use as they see fit. On the other hand, to the extent the unregulated operations make use of facilities the costs of which have been recovered by depreciation charges to purchasers of the regulated services—or, more generally, that the companies realize capital gains by selling for more than net book value assets that have been included in rate base[112]—there is a sense in which

---

[112] One issue in the afore-mentioned proceeding involving the petition of SNET for reorganization was the price at which the "retail assets" of the parent ILEC were to be transferred to the unregulated retail subsidiary. The Connecticut Department's Office of Consumer Council (OCC), asserting that if those assets were offered in the open market they would be worth a great deal more than net book value, contended that they should be transferred at market value, giving purchasers of regulated services the benefit of the difference; and that was the position ultimately taken by the Department:

> the economic cost to SAI [the unregulated retail affiliate] and SNET for the associated [Telco] assets will be the depreciated book value or retail market value, whichever is higher ....

op. cit., p. 56. This accords with my own conception of regulatory precedent. Purchasers of regulated services would, indeed, be entitled, under original cost regulation, to any capital gains—the difference between depreciated acquisition costs and sales prices—on any assets sold or otherwise transferred; the same would seem to apply to assets transferred to an unregulated affiliated entity. It would seem only equitable that the benefit of the difference between net book and market value accrue to the purchasers of the regulated services, who had paid more for those services what turned out to be the actual cost of serving them. See, along the same lines, the recent decision by the New York State Public Service Commission to require Bell Atlantic to return to New York customers the net proceeds from its sale of Bell Communications Research (Bellcore) attributable to the New York region:

> since Bell Atlantic's interest in Bellcore has been funded by ratepayers, there is no doubt that the net proceeds of this sale should be returned to ratepayers,

the Commission declared. (Press Release, Nov. 5, 1997.)

It would also be difficult to quarrel with the OCC's proposed application of that

continued...)

that differential really "belongs" to the purchasers of the regulated services, so long as their commissions have operated consistently on an
original cost or prudent investment basis for determining allowable revenues.[113] This proposition is the corollary of the entitlement of the utility
companies to recovery of their stranded costs. The measure of those
costs and that entitlement is, precisely, the extent to which the market
value of the companies' assets falls short of their book value.

The efficient solution to the treatment of the costs of new investments in
multi-purpose facilities capable of supplying regulated and unregulated
services together—and the only one fully compatible with the intention
of the Telecommunications Act to establish a "pro-competitive, deregulatory national policy framework designed to accelerate rapidly private
sector deployment of advanced telecommunications and information
technologies,"[114] while sheltering purchasers of the regulated services

---

(*...continued*)

precedent to the SNET reorganization on grounds of the prerequisites of efficient
competition. Requiring SNET to credit purchasers of its regulated services with those
capital gains would not handicap it in its competition with others on a going-forward
basis. Indeed, if a utility company were to be permitted to carry over to its competitive operations assets that would in effect give it an unjustifiable advantage over rivals
by saving it incremental investment costs that others would have to undertake, ex-
tracting that advantage for the benefit of regulated rates would not illegitimately
handicap it in that competition.

[113] On the other hand, SNET's regulated services collectively (but far from uniformly)
have historically been underpriced by virtue of what has generally been conceded
were depreciation rates that fell short of the losses in economic value of its assets.
In these circumstances, both equity and economic efficiency would suggest that
the benefit of the difference between book costs and market value of the "retail assets" claimed by the Office of Consumer Counsel be used not to reduce further the
prices of regulated services collectively but to make good the accumulated consequence of inadequate depreciation in the past—that is to say, to write down the remaining assets of the successor wholesale ILEC toward market value.

This is, indeed, what the Department decided: "All proceeds associated with the
transfer will be credited to the reserve deficiency of the Telco." *Ibid.*

[114] *Telecommunications Act of 1996 Conference Report*, S. Rep., 104-230 at 113 (Feb.
1, 1996); also par. 1.

from the risks and costs of such ventures—not only requires no cost allocations but is almost certainly likely to be frustrated by them. It is to leave the course of regulated rates unaffected by those ventures, in either direction. This would have the automatic consequence of forcing stockholders of the companies to bear the entire cost, including the risk of loss, while also ensuring their full retention of whatever net profits they are able to reap in this way.

Such a result could especially easily be achieved in the majority of states that (along with the FCC) regulate on the basis of rate caps rather than cost-plus or rate base/rate of return.[115] With rates already set on their course—whether by simple freezes or multi-year indexations—all that is necessary is an agreement by a commission not to change those caps or formulas in consideration of these multi-purpose investments. The danger of commissions engaging instead in kleptocratic allocations of these costs was clearly signaled by the FCC's declaration of intention that "at least some of the benefit of the economy of scope between telephony and competitive services"[116] ought to accrue to purchasers of the former.[117] It has a plausible ring—indeed, an element of validity—entirely apart from considerations of fairness. There is no economic principle that dictates conferring all the benefits of economies of scope on the purchases of new services in situations in which rates for all services set uniformly at incremental costs would fail to recover total costs. On the other hand, economic efficiency and efficient competition dictate that all investments be undertaken the anticipated revenues from which recover the full incremental (and only those incremental) costs. If regulators divert some of those revenues for the benefit of purchasers of preexisting, regulated services, while not allocating to them a corresponding proportion

---

[115] According to NERA count, at least 30 states had done so as of the end of 1996.

[116] *In the Matter of Allocation of Costs Associated with Local Carrier Exchange Provision of Video Programming Services*, CC Docket No. 96-112, *Notice of Proposed Rulemaking*, May 10, 1996 (NPRM), par. 23.

[117] The FCC signalled a similar attempt to treat "all such reallocations [of costs] to non-regulated activities ... [as exogenous cost changes that would] trigger decreases in related price cap indexes." (*Ibid.*, at par. 60)

of the incremental costs, it can not but discourage efficient new ventures that would otherwise be undertaken.[118]

Similar distortions are created by the frequent demands of commissions—urged upon them by representatives of both customers and competitors—for:

- "royalty" payments by the utility companies in exchange for permission to engage in unregulated operations, typically unaccompanied by symmetrical sharing by ratepayers in any losses the companies might suffer in those operations;

- requirements that exchanges of goods and services between utility and unregulated operations be priced asymmetrically—at allocated costs or market value, whichever is higher, for transfers in one direction and at allocated costs or market value, whichever is lower, in the opposite[119];

- transfer rules such as were proposed in both California and in New York (in the latter case in the Commission's code of conduct for

---

[118] I have expounded this argument at length in my "How to Treat the Costs of Shared Voice and Video Networks in a Post-regulatory Age," *Policy Analysis*, #264, Nov. 27, 1996, Cato Institute. As to the consideration that in the presence of economies of scale and scope, such as it is envisioned the ILECs would be seeking to exploit in these ventures, rates for the several services would have to exceed incremental costs if company operations were to be sustainable in the aggregate:

- efficient markups on the unregulated services would presumably be small, because of the relative elasticity of market demand for them and

- because of their even greater elasticity of demand from the standpoint of the ILEC, because they are likely to be subject to competitive offerings (e.g., from cable TV operators). Finally,

- it is clearly more consistent with the unregulated competition that is the goal of the Act to leave it to the several suppliers to get their markups where and as their various markets allow, with the role of regulators confined to seeing to it they do not get them by shifting risks or costs to purchasers of the still-regulated services.

[119] The latter requirement, standing alone, is a familiar, efficient regulatory practice, as a means of preventing regulated companies from exploiting their captive customers by pricing inputs supplied to them by unregulated affiliates at higher-than-competitive levels.

the ConEd restructuring plan) that would require a compensation equivalent to 25 percent of base pay for employees transferred to unregulated operations, or, again in California, adding 5 percent of direct labor cost to fully loaded costs on transfers of goods and services from utilities to unregulated affiliates—all of them excessively generous to ratepayers and, for the same reason, inefficiently burdensome on utility company competition and protective of competitors.

Considerations of pure economic efficiency would require that any such transfers be at bare marginal or incremental costs.[120] That would be the measure of the costs of supplying those inputs to the affiliates imposed on the utility company and its ratepayers; it would insure against those customers being in any way burdened by those operations and enable the affiliates to apply the full economies of scope to their competitive efforts.

From this standpoint, a requirement instead that the transfers be at fully allocated, average costs would be unduly generous to patrons of the regulated operations and inefficiently protective of competitors. At the same time, it has the attractiveness, from the regulatory perspective, of permitting purchasers of the utility services to share proportionately in the benefits of those economies, which service to them has made possible. It has the additional attractiveness of administrative convenience and unequivocal effectiveness in protecting both competitors and utility customers from cross-subsidization. If there is one thing that regulators are good at—too effective, indeed, in protecting purchasers of regulated services and competitors—it is allocating costs. None of my severe criticisms of those allocations has denied their efficacy in achieving their intended purposes; it is the purposes—for which the allocations are a rationalization—that merit disapproval.[121]

---

[120] I set aside here, but discuss at several points elsewhere, the fact that charges for access to essential facilities might have to exceed that level (subject to the efficient component pricing rule), in order to permit recovery of regulatorily imposed costs and to equalize the competition between utility and unregulated companies.

[121] In this connection, the Federal Communication Commission has now officially found that its various accounting safeguards, including its existing rules governing

(*continued...*)

In light of these considerations, I see absolutely no justification for the rules going even beyond in the ways to which I have alluded. The requirement of a ransom payment for transferring employees cannot be justified by the familiar regulatory requirement that if assets are sold at prices above net book value, ratepayers are entitled to the difference.[122] No such reasoning is applicable to the transfer of employees, on the basis of the analogy that ratepayers have similarly paid for the accumulation of experience that has made them more valuable than they would otherwise be. Purchasers pay the costs of employees' services when they receive them; they do not by so doing acquire an equity stake in the employees themselves—nor could they, under the Thirteenth Amendment to the U.S. Constitution.[123]

While full cost allocations, resulting in pricing inputs supplied by the utility company to its unregulated operations markedly above the bare

---

(*...continued*)

transactions between the LECs and affiliates, are fully sufficient to guard against subsidization of competitive activities at the expense of subscribers to regulated telecommunications services. *Report and Order, In the Matter of Implementation of the Telecommunications Act of 1996: Accounting Safeguards*, FCC 96-490, CC Docket No. 96-150, adopted Dec. 23, 1996, pars. 1, 25, 108 and 275.

[122] A consideration in the prices paid for utility companies or portions of them may well be the value not just of their physical assets but of the goodwill associated with those assets and/or of the teams of experienced workers, already assembled, that are expected to go with them. Any consequent excess of the purchase price over the net book value of the assets would, under the regulatory doctrine I have already described and endorsed, accrue to the utility's customers.

[123] The compensation that beginning or relatively inexperienced workers receive may be conceived of as consisting of two parts—the current wage and the accumulating experience that offers the prospect of higher wages in the future. Both of these belong to them, as a matter of both economics and equity. I have yet to see the advocates of a ransom payment by the affiliated entities for workers transferred to them from utility companies contend that purchasers of utility services should be empowered to collect that same ransom when the employees transfer to unaffiliated competitors. Yet the effect of the ransom price for employees prescribed by the California standards would be to give those competitors of the utility company a 25 percent-of-one-year's-salary advantage over its own affiliates in attracting such workers. Such a consequence might comport with the competitive handicapping of incumbent utilities that seems to be the essential purpose of these rules; but it accords with no principle of efficient competition of which I am aware.

incremental costs that pure economic efficiency and efficient competition would dictate, may serve as a rough-and-ready way of permitting purchasers of the regulated services to share "equitably" in the economies of scope, they will, predictably, not satisfy the complaints by competitors that the resulting competition is "unfair."[124]

C. TELRIC-BS

The most flagrant recent examples of presumptuous regulatory micro-management of what purports to be a process of deregulation and of combined timidity and disingenuousness in establishing the conditions for true deregulation have emerged from the three major proceedings that the FCC undertook in 1996 to promulgate rules effectuating the Telecommunications Act of that year. These involve:

(1) setting the terms and conditions under which the ILECs are to be required to make unbundled parts of their facilities and retail services available to competitors;[125]

(2) reforming the access charges to long-distance carriers for originating and terminating long distance calls;[126] and

(3) designing a system of explicit subsidies to ensure universality of subscription to telephone service, financed in such a way as no

---

[124] For example, a witness for the Delaware Office of Public Advocate objected to the proposed 24-cent charge by Delmarva Power & Light to its unregulated operations as their share of the cost of sending customers a monthly bill—the result of a 50/50 allocation of the billing costs between regulated and unregulated services—as conferring an "unfair" advantage on Delmarva's competitive services, even though the incremental costs would be only a small fraction of that amount, because billing would cost competitors at least 32 cents. Direct Testimony of Andrea C. Crane in Delaware PSC, Docket No. 97-65 (supra, note 35).

[125] *Interconnection Order*, note 62, above.

[126] It is necessary to add at once, in fairness, that the Commission has, in its decision of May 7, 1997, in this proceeding, shown some recognition of the dangers of the course it embarked on in the first one and some tendency to pull back from it. See section III.C.3.

longer to distort competition by creating opportunities for competitors to undercut the incumbents in offering the subsidizing services, and also, by making good the difference between the suppressed basic residential rates and the actual costs of providing that service, to encourage facilities-based competition in offering it.

1. Unbundled network elements

With respect to the first of these, the law requires only that the charges for those inputs be "based on cost" and "may include a reasonable profit," as I have already pointed out. In consideration of (a) the fact that economically efficient rates would be based on marginal or incremental rather than average or historical costs[127] and (b) the likelihood, in its opinion, that the costs of the telephone companies, regulated hitherto on a cost-plus basis, reflect inefficiencies, the FCC has prescribed that the rates they charge for network elements be based to some vaguely prescribed extent[128] on a version of the long-run incremental costs of the entire unbundled network element demanded—TELRIC— in which "long-run" is employed in the theoretical economic sense of a time perspective in which all costs are variable and minimized.[129] Some of the rivals or

---

[127] The law provides additional justification for the FCC ignoring the traditional basis for commissions setting utility companies' "revenue requirements" by stipulating that costs are to be "determined without reference to a rate-of-return or other rate-based proceeding." The Act, Sec. 252 (d)(1)(A).

[128] The Commission clearly envisions the incorporation of some mark-ups above TELRIC for these network components, although it explicitly contends that—in contrast with the several telecommunications *services*—those components or elements have relatively few common costs, which would have to be recovered via such mark-ups. The Commission also concedes the need at some point to determine to what extent the ILECs are to be entitled to mark-ups toward the recovery of their sunk costs, although in the charges for which services it has not yet made clear.

[129] The Commission's TELRIC represents a compromise between the estimated incremental costs that the ILECs will actually incur and the costs of a totally new system built from scratch, by stipulating that the hypothetical system take as given the current location of the wire centers of the incumbent LECs. In so doing, it has

(continued...)

would-be rivals of the LECs and staffs of some utility commissions have demanded much less equivocally than the FCC that the rates be set *at* that level—the total costs of a hypothetical, most-efficient new entrant, writing, as it were, on a blank slate: hence, my application to it of the acronym TSLRIC-BS. Such rates would of course include no provision for the recovery of historical or sunk costs—return on and of past investments, depreciated hitherto at unrealistically low rates.

The advocacy of TSLRIC-BS is based on the assumption that this is the level to which effective competition would drive prices.[130] That view is mistaken.

In a world of continuous technological progress, it would be irrational for firms constantly to update their facilities in order *completely* to incorporate today's lowest-cost technology, as though starting from scratch, the moment those costs fell below prevailing market prices. Investments made today, totally embodying the most modern technology available currently, would instantaneously be outdated tomorrow and, in consequence, fail over their lifetime to earn a return sufficient to justify the investments in the first place. For this reason, as Professor William J. Fellner pointed out many years ago,[131] firms even in competitive industries would systematically practice what he termed "anticipatory retardation." In other words, they would adopt the most modern technology

---

(*...continued*)

  explicitly rejected proposals by the ILECs that the rates be "based on" their own projected actual incremental costs as variants of the "embedded cost" approach traditionally employed by regulatory commissions in setting rates. As we will see, it forthrightly adopts the hypothetical TSLRIC-BS concept, however, as one of the legs (the other being actual regulatorily-prescribed *rates*) for determining the universal service subsides for which LECs would be qualified. *In the Matter of Access Charge Reform*, CC Docket No. 26-262 et al, *First Report and Order*, May 7, 1997 (hereafter *Access Reform Order*, 97-158), par. 381.

[130] See the *Interconnection Order*, par. 683.

[131] "The Influence of Market Structure on Technological Progress," in American Economic Association, *Readings in Industrial Organization and Public Policy* (Homewood: Richard D. Irwin, 1958), as described also in my *The Economics of Regulation*, Vol. 1, pp. 199-200, note 91.

only when the progressively declining real costs had fallen sufficiently below currently prevailing prices to offer them a reasonable expectation of earning a return on those investments over their economic lives.

Two other ways of putting this proposition would be that:

- competitive prices will in such situations typically exceed TSLRIC-BS (or, in the case of a single-product firm, the average total costs of a new production facility) by a substantial margin;[132] or

- firms would incur the heavy sunk costs of investing in totally new facilities, embodying the most recent technology from the ground up, only if prevailing market prices were high enough to provide rapid depreciation of those costs and rates of return that Jerry Hausman has estimated would have to be two to three times current costs of capital.[133]

Observe the presumption that this proposal reflects. The Commission has in effect declared: "*We* will determine not what your costs are or will be but what we think they *ought to be*. Why should we bother to let the messy and uncertain competitive process determine the outcome when *we* can determine at the very outset what those results would be and prescribe them now?" [134]

---

[132] This would be so entirely apart from the necessity, in the case of multi-product producers, of markups above incremental costs, in the presence of economies of scope, in order to permit recovery of total costs.

[133] Affidavit of USTA Comments, *Implementation of the Local Competition Provisions of the Telecommunications Act of 1996*, CC Docket No. 96-98, May 16, 1996. See also Richard Schmalensee and William E. Taylor, "Economic Aspects of Access Reform: A Reply," NERA USTA Reply Comments, CC Docket No. 96-262, Feb. 14, 1997. The FCC has, in terms that could be characterized only as grudging, recognized the possibility that it would be necessary to incorporate higher-than-customary rates of depreciation and return in these calculations for this very reason. *Interconnection Order*, par. 686.

[134] Dennis L. Weisman characterizes what the FCC has done here as "confusing mandating the competitive outcome with fostering the competitive process." "The (In)Efficiency of the Efficient Firm Cost Standard," Ms., Jan. 1998, p. 4. The presumption on the part of the FCC was evidently jurisdictional as well as substantive. See the reference to the rebuke administered by the Circuit Court of Appeals in note 135, immediately following, as well as to its previous decision holding that the Commission had exceeded its authority, note 16, above.

It takes little imagination or knowledge of regulatory history to envision the combat-by-engineering-and-econometric-models that the TSLRIC-BS standard has invited.[135] Its proponents clearly imply (and their proffered models purport to demonstrate) that it will provide a cost basis for ILEC charges lower than their own TSLRICs—that is, that the latter

---

[135] No one with any awareness of the history of the tortured efforts by utility commissions in the early decades of this century to comply with the Supreme Court's instruction that utility company rate bases take into account "the present as compared with the original cost of construction" could possibly have opened the door to similar exercises of "calculating" any BS version of incremental cost. As Ben W. Lewis described that experience:

> It is not too much to say that in terms of cost, delay, uncertainty, and the arousing of animosity and contention, the performance of the reproduction cost method falls little short of a public scandal; by far the greater part of the grotesque and costly ponderosity which characterizes modern rate regulation is to be attributed directly and solely to the reproduction cost approach. There is no occasion here to recite details of the maneuvering in a typical rate proceeding. The months and years spent by contending parties, commissions, and courts over such hypothetical factors as pricing, conditions of construction, labor performance, overheads, intangibles; the huge sums paid to engineers and accountants and other professional experts, directed in their claims and counterclaims by high-priced attorneys skilled in the art of rate case strategy; the highly charged, politico-legal-mystic character of the whole performance—this is all accepted practice under the reproduction cost method ...

Leverett S. Lyon and Victor Abramson, *Government and Economic Life: Development and Current Issues of American Public Policy*, Washington: Brookings, 1940, Vol. 2, p. 691.

If only Ben Lewis were alive today, it would have been a delight to have his report on the negotiations and arbitrations, numbering in the thousands, being conducted before utility commissions all over the country, under instructions to ascertain the TSLRIC-BS of network elements. As George Santayana said, "Those who cannot remember the past are condemned to repeat it."

Ironically, Reed Hundt, Chairman of the FCC that adopted the TELRIC-BS "methodogy" in these several decisions—to the point of ultimately eliciting from the 8th Circuit Court of Appeals a writ of mandamus against its continued efforts to force it on the state commissions (Iowa Utilities Board et. al. v FCC, Order on motions for enforcement of the mandate, filed Jan. 22, 1998)—was reported, after leaving the Commission, as saying

> he never really has liked use of models that 'aren't based on the real world' and he's not picking on any particular model: 'I'm criticizing them all.' Asked later when he had become so skeptical about models, he said he always had been 'internally.' *Communications Daily*, Feb., 11, 1998, pp. 2-3.

costs embody inefficiencies that would be avoided by a hypothetical totally new network. If that factual premise were indeed valid, efficiency would require that the incumbent company be totally replaced, instantaneously, by a wholly new venture or scrap its entire existing plant and start over from the ground—strictly, in view of the FCC's qualification of the blank slate, from the wire center[136]—up. If regulators really believed the results those models are producing, they would be derelict in their duty if they did not order the ILECs instantaneously to do exactly that. There is every reason to believe, therefore, that the tendency for some proxy models introduced in arbitration and state regulatory proceedings purporting to measure TELRIC coming out consistently lower than the estimates by the LECs of their own incremental costs is the consequence, at least in part, of their applying traditional regulatorily determined rates of depreciation and costs of capital, which would, for the reasons we have already given, be grossly insufficient to induce investors to construct entirely new systems from scratch.[137] For this very reason, considerations of economic efficiency and efficient competition alone *require* that the prices charged to competitors be based upon the LECs' *actual* costs, including realistic depreciation rates and costs of capital appropriate to the changed regulatory climate. To the extent competitors can provide these inputs more efficiently than the LECs, this will fully preserve their incentive to do so and thereby promote efficient facilities-based entry.

---

[136] See note 129, above.

[137] In further demonstration of the mismatch between the hypothetical "measure" and the way incremental costs are actually incurred in the real world, one exponent of these models attributed to telephone service only one quarter of the cost of poles and other conduits, on the grounds that in a system newly constructed from scratch, a much larger portion would be used for electric and cable service than is actually used today. The blank slate assumption evidently requires, logically, that these other, non-telephone companies be assumed to be writing on such a slate as well. Hatfield Model Release 3.1, Model Description, Hatfield Associates, Inc., Feb. 28, 1997, Appendix B, p. 52. John Donovan, head of the Hatfield model engineering group, has admitted that this was the assumption on which they operated, but that they took the configurations of the cities in which these facilities would be placed as they are today:

> MR. DONOVAN: In this model we assume forward-looking technology with efficient firms and we assume that co-occupants will be just as efficient as we are in this model, so ... we assumed that whether it's through mechanized databases

(continued...)

That, of course, is exactly how competition works. The solution most compatible with leaving it to the market to weed out X-inefficiencies (so-named precisely because no one can know their dimensions *a priori*—the very case for regulators refraining from presuming to do so) is (1) to begin with existing, regulatorily prescribed rates, (2) so long as competition is insufficiently intense, to regulate the pertinent services by application of price caps, accompanied with a downward productivity adjustment, calculated as fairly as possible[137a]; and (3) to open the

---

(*...continued*)

or good coordination meetings that if cable TV, the power company, local telephone company and even another provider want to use the same valuable structure that they will operate efficiently and be out there at the same time and not hold each other up.

MR. POTTER: So in effect you're assuming that the cities are as they exist today but all of the utilities are building their respective networks anew at the same time.

MR. DONOVAN: Yes.

And, again:

MR. CARNALL: I want to be sure that you are clear that you're assuming that all the utilities are building at the same time?

MR. DONOVAN: That's correct.

MR. CARNALL: So this is scorched everybody not just scorched telephone?

MR. DONOVAN: Correct.

Washington Utilities and Transportation Commission, *In the Matter of the Pricing Proceeding for Interconnection, Unbundled Elements, Transport and Termination, and Resale*, Docket No. UT-960369, et al., Workshop, Feb. 14, 1997, pp. 00188-89.

One wonders why the witness did not carry this scenario to the logical conclusion by positing entire urban areas with streets and all other public facilities built on a green field in such a way as to minimize all the costs of all the services they would be used to provide; and a country with its entire educational system re-designed so as to provide—or to *have* provided—a labor force optimally adapted to today's configuration of technologies and consumer demands. It would be difficult to conceive of a more apt illustration of Keynes' classic observation that "in the long run we are all dead."

[137a] For a description of the remarkable experience with the price caps applied to British Telecom, indexed to the retail price index, under which the so-called X factor (the annual productivity adjustment) was increased in steps from 3 percent to 7.5 percent over the short span of a decade—a 40 percent

(*continued...*)

market to competition—protected by rules of competitive parity or efficient component pricing—to force prices to efficient levels.

In unregulated markets, prices tend to be set on the basis of the actual costs of incumbent firms, and they should be. The economic purpose of prices set at incremental cost is to inform buyers—and make them pay—the cost that society will *actually* incur if they purchase more or would *actually* save if they reduced their purchases, entirely or partially. These can only be the costs of the supplier whose prices are being set, not some hypothetical ideal producer. Moreover, such prices give challengers the proper target at which to shoot—the proper standard to meet or beat and the proper reward if they succeed. If they can achieve costs lower than that, they will enter and *in the process* (which the FCC's pricing rules would omnisciently short-circuit) beat prices down to efficient levels. In contrast, TELRIC-based charges—if the FCC's apparent expectation that such rates would be lower than rates based on the telephone companies' actual costs is correct—would actually discourage competitors coming in and building their own facilities, which it was the clear intention of the new Act to encourage.[138]

2. Wholesale rates

The Commission engaged in a similar act of presumption—as well as violation of the principles of efficient competition—in the method it prescribed for determining the discounts from their retail prices at which the ILECs are to be required to offer their retail services to resellers.

(...*continued*)

decline in rates, in real terms, while the Company continued to earn a consistently high rate of return—see Vogelsang and Mitchell, *op. cit.*, pp. 269-76 and 296.

[138] Dennis Weisman has pointed out another intriguing consequence of the TSLRIC-BS standard. Since it is inconceivable that an ILEC would be permitted to reduce the prices of its competitive services below the floor of *its own* incremental costs, rates for unbundled elements of its own network set by regulators at the lower, hypothetical level open up the fascinating likelihood of ILECs being forced, in effect,

(*continued...*)

The Telecommunications Act calls for discounts equated to the "costs that will be avoided" by the ILECs (Sec. 252 (d)(3))—which can mean only the costs that they would *actually* avoid in selling the services at wholesale. The FCC, instead, calls for a discount equated to "all of the costs that the LEC incurs in maintaining a retail, as opposed to whole-sale, business." (*Interconnection Order*, par. 911). These two concepts are obviously very different. The costs that an ILEC will avoid by sell-ing *some portion* of a service at wholesale rather than at retail (i.e., the LRIC of some increment or decrement of its total retail sales smaller than the total) will undoubtedly be smaller, on a per unit basis, than if it were to abandon retailing entirely (thereby saving the LRIC of the entire service). This difference is a reflection of economies of scale or scope. The costs added or saved by taking on or giving up a portion of the total output of a service or group of services are lower than the (average) in-cremental costs of their entire output. It undoubtedly explains the differ-ence between the discounts well below 10 percent at least originally advocated by ILECs and the 17-25 percent stipulated by the FCC.

The question is, which of the two should prevail if competition is to be efficient?

Manifestly—I allude here to the example used by Professors Kaserman and Mayo[139]—if the ILECs save only $2 a unit in retailing cost by selling some of their output of a service at wholesale rather than retail but are required by the FCC and state commissions, which seem generally to have followed the FCC's instructions, to offer a discount of $5, it will encourage the entry of resellers whose additional costs of performing that function exceed the costs society will save by having the incumbents cease to perform it.[140]

(...*continued*)

    to *undercut themselves*—by selling network elements to rivals at prices below their own incremental costs—and at the same time prohibited by the injunction against predation from meeting the rates of rivals *using their own facilities*. Direct Testimony on behalf of Southwestern Bell before the Texas Public Utilities Commission, Docket Nos. 16189 *et al.*, Sept. 15, 1997, pp. 4, 9-10 and *op. cit.*, note 134, above, pp. 9-16.

[139] *Loc. cit.*, note 68, above.

[140] This means that a required discount based on the TSLRIC of retailing, which Pro-fessors Kaserman and Mayo explicitly approve, will not, in fact, ensure efficient competition, as they assert. The FCC and they have both misspecified the relevant increment, violating these principles set forth in note 101, above.

What we have here is another example of incumbent companies being forced to give up some of the benefits of economies of scale or scope, in the interest of encouraging the entry of competitors, even if they are less efficient.

But how can resellers be expected to enter if the total cost per unit of efficient retailing is $5 a unit and they have to operate within a $2 discount? The answer is that they should not enter in that event because their costs *for the relevant increment* exceed those of the incumbents.

Recall, moreover, my assertion that denying incumbents the advantages of economies of scale or scope is unacceptable in terms not only of theory but of the likely factual circumstances—i.e., the likelihood that no competitors will have access to economies comparable to those available to the incumbents. As I have pointed out, these economies, which tend to produce lower average costs for partial increments than for entire services, are likely to be available to the major challengers of the ILECs as well. Such potential competitors at the local level as the existing long-distance carriers, cable companies and resellers of long-distance services *are themselves already engaged in retailing*. The costs to them of adding local services to their present mix will therefore similarly be lower than the total per-unit cost of engaging in retailing as compared with not engaging in retailing. If they are not lower, those companies should not, in fact, be encouraged to enter—certainly not by regulators requiring that they be offered discounts greater than the ILECs would actually save by selling to them at wholesale.[141]

---

[141] It might appear that the presence of hundreds of resellers of long-distance telephone service, whom regulators have guaranteed no wholesale discounts at all, attests to the lack of need even of pure resellers for discounts other than those already incorporated in the retail price schedules of the ILECs. See note 67, above. That inference would probably be unjustified. The keen competition in the long-distance market for large business customers—even before MCI entered it, AT&T found it necessary to offer deep discounts in order to prevent them from installing their own private microwave systems—opened up a wide margin for arbitrage (between the deeply discounted prices for large-volume purchases and the charges to smaller customers) once AT&T was forbidden to deny those discounts to resellers. It does not appear that the growing competition at the local level for business accounts in concentrated metropolitan areas has opened up similar opportunities.

The foregoing argument has been directed against the FCC's decision to prescribe wholesale discounts greater than the actual avoided costs of the incumbent LECs. Neither, of course, should they be smaller. To the extent the prescribed discounts follow this prescription, they will ensure against the ILECs recovering the costs of inefficiencies in their retailing operations such as they may have accumulated under historical cost-plus regulation. Such a discount would establish a retail margin within which any equally efficient competing retailer—with efficiency defined, of course, in terms of the costs of the increments of output *actually at stake*—could survive. In this way, the wholesale price compatible with efficient competition would be reached without the need for regulatory determinations of the costs of a hypothetical ideally efficient competitor. It could safely be left to competition thereafter to *determine* the *efficient* markup. Manifestly, entrants with incremental retailing costs lower than those of the putatively inefficient incumbents could prosper.

3. Carrier access charges

Possibly (indeed, one would hope) in response to criticisms such as these, the Commission has—for a transition period—abandoned what it calls the "prescriptive approach" to the reform of carrier access charges, which would have involved its setting those rates (just as it has presumed to set the rates for unbundled network elements) forthwith at "economically efficient" levels, in favor of a "market-based" approach. This means, as it declares in its *Access Charge Reform* and *Price Cap Performance Review* decisions, leaving the determination of efficient charges to competition and, so long as competition is insufficient, to rate caps with a recalculated X or productivity factor—following precisely the logic of my foregoing argument.[142]

At the same time, its self-denying ordinance is far from permanent. Its reason for rejecting the immediate prescription of TSLRIC-BS is that "accurate forward-looking cost models are not available at the present time to determine the economic costs of providing access service" (par. 45). The

---

[142] *Access Reform Order,* 97-158, pars. 7 and 44 and text at note 137a, above.

Order therefore directs the LECs to develop such studies and be prepared to present them for possible adoption by Feb. 8, 2001, if it determines that "competition is not developing sufficiently for the market-based approach to work." (par. 48)

Moreover, Paul Vasington has pointed out to me, this declaration of intention raises an intriguing prospect. Presumably the FCC will at that time decide whether the competitive process has worked by comparing access charges with the costs produced by these TSLRIC-BS studies, which it has endorsed in principle. But if, as we have argued, the competitive process will not produce such prices (except if they include depreciation rates and costs of capital reflecting the pertinent risks in much fuller measure than the FCC seems to have recognized), it looks as though the Commission has committed itself in advance to finding, in 2001, that the market-based approach has failed and to reverting to a full prescriptive approach—that is, one in which it would itself set the charges at "efficient" levels.

What is satisfying about this more recent decision is that in opting for the market-based approach, in combination with a revised price cap formula (albeit perhaps only until it thinks it will have perfected its prescriptive capabilities—a regulatory oxymoron), the Commission all but explicitly adopts the logic of my foregoing criticisms of its fondness for TSLRIC-BS as the basis for charges for unbundled inputs—namely, that competition is the more reliable determinant of efficient rates and that regulatory prescription of rates could distort investment decisions by competitive entrants. It also recognizes that reliance by competitive LECs (CLECs) on switched access services, on the one hand, and unbundled inputs of the incumbents, on the other, are in some measure alternative methods of originating and terminating calls, and that its application of differing cost standards could distort the CLECs' choices between them. (See pars. 262-65)

What is discouraging, by the same reasoning, is:

(1) the Commission's failure to recognize that these same criticisms apply equally to its manifest fondness for prescribing TSLRIC-BS-based rates for unbundled network elements and for the

mandatory wholesale discounts on sales for resale, in preference to rates based on the actual LRICs of the incumbent LECs;

(2) its promise to revert to that same prescriptive standard for access charges by 2001; and

(3) its failure to realize that its prescription of TSLRIC-BS for network elements conflicts with the logic of its refusal to prescribe similar bare incremental-cost-based charges for carrier access—namely, that it would subvert the inherited rate structure before alternative mechanisms for supporting basic residential rates had been put into place—a conflict we will explore further in Part IV.C.

4. The effect on competitive investment and innovation

As the foregoing considerations demonstrate, the proposed TSLRIC-BS standard for unbundled network elements and carrier access charges and, even more egregiously, for wholesale discounts on sales for resale strongly discourages genuinely facilities-based competition. What is the point of a CLEC constructing its own facilities if it can lease or purchase them from the incumbent companies at the theoretically estimated *minimum* cost (let alone below that cost, for the reasons I have already adduced) that would be incurred by a new entrant building from the ground up? What is the point if it can simply buy whatever retail services it wishes to offer from them at a wholesale discount estimated by the regulators to be sufficient (actually, as I have pointed out, more than sufficient) to enable an equally efficient retailer to compete?[143] In competitive markets, we have already observed, prices tend to be set on the

---

[143] The FCC acknowledges that: "[blank slate TELRIC] may discourage facilities-based competition by new entrants because new entrants can use the incumbent LEC's existing network based on the cost of a hypothetical least-cost, most efficient network." *Interconnection Order* (Docket 96-98), par. 683. See also Gerald W. Brock, "Local Competition Policy Maneuvers," *Selected Papers from the 1996 Telecommunications Policy Research Conference*, pp. 10-12. Brock offers other criticisms of the FCC's proposed TELRIC basis for the pricing of network elements that are echoed elsewhere in this paper. For example,

(*continued...*)

basis of the costs of the incumbent companies. These give challengers the proper target to try to meet or beat and the full reward, to the extent their costs prove to be lower than those of the incumbents. But, of course, if regulators are wise enough to be able to prescribe the results competition would produce, there is no need for competition.

What is particularly troublesome about the FCC's proposals is that its conception of the prerequisites for achieving efficiency is entirely *static*, while competition—especially in telecommunications—is inherently dynamic. Any proposal that rates be set at costs, or cost plus regulatorily-prescribed markups, should at least, in consideration of the critical importance of innovation, distinguish the rules applicable to existing network elements or to sales of existing retail services for resale from the rules that would apply to new ones. To tie the rates for new services closely to costs, incremental or otherwise, would fatally attenuate the incentives of incumbents to develop new and innovative services (as I have already argued in Part II.D), as well as of competitors to enter on a facilities basis.[144]

The historical institution of tightly regulated, franchised monopolies

---

(...*continued*)

> The many uncertainties in computing forward looking incremental cost make it seem that TELRIC is a poor substitute for existing regulatory mechanisms. There are likely to be many disputes over the standards for those components and there is no simple self-correcting mechanism attached to them. This order places more confidence in the cost allocation methodology required to compute TELRIC prices than I believe is warranted from the past experience with cost allocation rules....TELRIC pricing of unbundled elements will require detailed knowledge and intervention to settle disputes and could lead to a substantial expansion of regulatory oversight. The TELRIC pricing for unbundled elements could diminish the progress made over the last decade in adopting incentive based regulation and return to a focus on company specific cost data. I don't see a natural path from the requirements of this order toward deregulation of the local exchange as competition increases, (p. 12).

[144] For a powerful argument blaming regulation for retarding investment in telecommunications infrastructure, see Duesterberg and Gordon, *op. cit.*, pp. 12-21 and *passim.* Also Robert G. Harris and C. Jeffrey Kraft, "Meddling Through: Regulating Local Telephone Competition in the United States," *Journal of Economic Perspectives*, Vol. 11 (Fall 1997), pp. 107-08.

lacked competitive stimuli to innovation.[145] But in offering those monopolists reasonable assurances that they would be permitted to recover their *total* prudently incurred investment costs—of unsuccessful as well as successful ventures—it did have a positive effect on their willingness and ability to innovate. As we have moved from cost-plus to a more competitively-oriented system of regulation, however, any requirement that charges to competitors for new network elements or services be closely tied to some tight measure of cost would destroy that previous symmetry. Rival entrants would then have the option of purchasing the results of successful innovation at bare cost, while leaving stranded the costs of unsuccessful ventures. Investors would be forced to absorb the costs of failed ventures—as in competitive markets generally—but denied the essential offsetting opportunity to reap whatever rewards the unregulated market would otherwise confer on ventures that turn out successfully.

---

[145] Rate base/rate of return regulation had a tendency also to discourage innovation that threatened to render existing facilities obsolete before they were fully depreciated. See my *The Economics of Regulation*, Vol. 1, pp. 117-22 ("Depreciation Policy and Technological Progress").

IV. The Assault on Carrier Access Charges

The Telecommunications Act's prescription that rates for unbundled inputs be based on cost plus, permissibly, "a reasonable profit" could clearly be construed to permit the incorporation of markups sufficient, along with the revenues from other still-overpriced services, to continue to provide the ILECs—which, it is worth reemphasizing, continue to be comprehensively regulated—a fair opportunity to recover their legitimate costs. These, of course, include the sunk costs associated with their scores of billions of dollars of investments inadequately recovered from ratepayers heretofore, along with the costs of ongoing, regulatorily prescribed cross-subsidizations.

The FCC makes only minimal allusion to these considerations in its proposed rules for the pricing of unbundled inputs, promising to "address that issue" in its upcoming proceeding on access charge reform (*Interconnection Order*, par. 707). Since the access charges the LECs impose on both inter- and intraLATA long-distance carriers, are, by universal concession, far above incremental costs[146] and they, along with the closely associated direct charges for long-distance services where they are allowed to provide it, account for by far the largest contribution toward the recovery of sunk costs and the costs of underpricing basic residential services,[147] it is not surprising that it is on the access charges and the FCC's proceedings on that subject that the issue has been most intensely joined.

MCI and AT&T have stridently demanded that those grossly inflated charges—which amount to some 40 percent of their total costs—be reduced promptly to incremental costs. The charges are, indisputably,

---

[146] In 1996 and 1997, the interstate access charges averaged perhaps 6 cents a minute (originating and terminating charges combined), incremental costs between 1/3 and 1/2 of one cent. See Haring and Rohlfs, "Economic Perspectives on Access Charge Reform," prepared for BellSouth Telecommunications, Jan. 29, 1997, and D. Kaserman, J. Mayo, M. Crew, N. Economides, G. Hubbard, D. Kleindorfer and C. Martins-Filho, "Local Competition Issues and the Telecommunications Act of 1996," prepared on behalf of AT&T, July 15, 1996, p. 27.

[147] See note 20, above.

irrational and inefficient, for two reasons. First, they perpetuate the gross allocative inefficiency consequent on the resulting overcharging for long-distance calls. Second, they artificially encourage bypass of the networks of the LECs, thereby generating an additional loss in productive efficiency, as customers, IXCs and competitors employ access mechanisms that cost more than those of the LECs but less than their rates.

In these circumstances, it is impossible not to be sympathetic with the mounting assault on them, even though it is in large measure hypocritical or ignorant. The most blatant hypocrisy was systematically exhibited by MCI's multi-million dollar advertising campaigns in late 1996 and early 1997, of which the following is a typical message:

> Local telephone monopolies are reaping billions of dollars in unjustified subsidies that they collect under the guise of beginning and ending your long-distance telephone calls. Those subsidies come straight from your pocket. Order the reduction of inflated access charges. Starting right now.[148]

Other MCI ads proclaimed that these charges produce "guaranteed monopoly profits for incumbents[149]" and advised consumers to phone the offending telephone companies and demand refunds. The corresponding ignorance was displayed also by an op-ed piece by Erik R. Olbeter and Lawrence Chimerine in the *New York Times*,[150] complaining on the one hand that "local phone service rates have not fallen" *and* calling for immediate reduction in carrier access charges.

What these assertions ignored or failed to perceive, willfully or otherwise, was:

---

[148] *New York Times*, Feb. 12, 1997, p. A 21. This hypocrisy is in no way mitigated by the fact that this particular advertisement consists largely in quotations from such organizations as the Competition Policy Institute, the AARP and the Consumer Federation of America.

[149] Op Ed page, *New York Times*, Oct. 28, 1996.

[150] "Revenge of the Baby Bells," Feb. 22, 1997, p. 21.

1. the direct historical and continuing causal connection between these two sets of charges, the one deliberately far above efficient levels in order to permit holding the other far below—a connection directly reflected, for example, in the courageous decision by the FCC, under its chairman Mark Fowler, back in June 1985, to impose a direct subscriber line charge—increasing gradually to the present $3.50 a month on residential bills—accompanied by a directly corresponding decrease in the carrier access charges; and[151]

2. the fact that the carrier access charge has always been directly regulated, explicitly set by utility commissions, including the FCC, at levels intented to be no higher than sufficient to afford the LECs a reasonable opportunity to recover their aggregate regulatorily determined revenue entitlements.[152]

A. The Likely Effect on Investment, Revisited

These various pieces of advice, therefore, unaccompanied by any suggestion that the FCC combine the recommended reduction in access

---

[151] See note 13, above.

[152] As I have already pointed out (see note 115, above), telephone rates in the majority of states, as well as at the federal level, are now regulated by application of price caps or simple price freezes, rather than on the traditional rate base/rate of return basis. The essence of the superiority of rate cap over the more traditional form of regulation is that, by eliminating the direct link between the costs of the regulated company and its rates, it provides much stronger incentives for improved efficiency—eliminating the familiar disincentive effects of cost-plus pricing. Under it, the companies are no longer, technically, entitled to rates that recover their costs. At the same time, those caps are usually set initially at levels determined—typically, in traditional rate case proceedings—to be "just and reasonable"—that is to say, at levels that afford the companies a reasonable opportunity to recover their total costs; and the course on which the price caps are set, typically incorporating a downward adjustment for improvements in productivity believed to be reasonably achievable, is one that, whether implicitly or by explicit finding of the regulators, will continue to provide an efficiently managed company a continuing opportunity to recover its costs.

charges with a further rebalancing between those rates and basic residential charges or settling on some alternative method of financing the cross-subsidization that they embody, constitute blatant invitations to kleptocratic behavior. In its *Access Charge Reform Order*, the FCC quite properly rebukes these advocates, citing its continuing obligation to ensure that rates are "just and reasonable"—albeit without explicitly pointing out that this obligation includes giving the regulated companies a fair chance of recovering their prudently incurred costs.[153]

The economic underpinning of traditional regulation was the recognition that if investors were promised a reasonable opportunity to recover those costs, the utilities' ability to attract capital would be ensured. No one can say with confidence what the effect would be on the ability of public utility companies, operating hitherto with this understanding, if those costs were now to be ignored and commissions were to base regulated rates instead on some such conception as TSLRIC-BS. This much, at least, seems undeniable. First, the experience of having had the rules of the regulatory game changed in such a way as to deny them recovery of costs that they had been entitled to recover under the preceding regulatory regime cannot but diminish their incentives to engage in such investments in the future.

Setting aside the consideration of equity, this might be regarded as a matter of indifference if any consequent reduction in investments by the incumbent companies in our telecommunications infrastructure could reliably be expected to be filled by new entrants. This would be particularly true if, never having been regulated from the outset, they faced no such possibility of the rules of the game being changed to their disadvantage in the future. On the other hand, to the extent that they were motivated to enter in part by the prospect of qualifying for governmentally dictated distributions from a universal service fund, the possibility of the

---

[153] "The market-based approach to access charge reform that we adopt will not, as some parties assert, expose customers of interstate access services to the unfettered exercise of market power. We will continue to maintain the current mechanisms upon which we rely to ensure that rates for these services are 'just and reasonable' ... " (par. 264, footnotes omitted)

government changing the rules of that distribution in the future would be likely to weigh more heavily on their current calculations if it had done so previously to the ILECs. In addition, as we have already observed, an FCC decision to set rates for network components and access services at bare cost—blank slate TSLRIC—cannot but discourage competitors from entering by constructing facilities of their own.

The likely depressing effect on investments in upgrading the public network of the recommended cut in access charges, uncompensated elsewhere, as well as of the FCC's proposed rates for network elements, is not confined to their effect on the *incentives* of both incumbent and competitive LECs. Even more directly and obviously, a reduction in the flow of revenues to them on the order of $15 billion (inter- and intrastate combined) annually could not but diminish drastically the *ability* of the former companies to finance such investments.[154]

---

[154] Some of these investments in on-going modernization could still be financed with external funds; but the higher cost of external financing via the capital markets would make some otherwise viable investment projects uneconomic. See Harold Bierman, Jr. and Jerome E. Hass, *An Introduction to Managerial Finance*, New York: Norton, 1973, p. 186; Kenneth A. Froot, David S. Sharfstein and Jeremy C. Stein, "A Framework for Risk Management," *Harvard Business Review*, Nov.-Dec. 1994, p. 94.

The order of magnitude of the decline in internal cash flows implied by TELRIC-BS-based charges for network elements in relation to the ongoing outlays of the companies is impressive. Southwestern Bell estimates, for example, that it would suffer a decline in its total revenues on the order of $285 million annually *if* all of its current customers were served with unbundled network elements priced at levels provisionally set by the Missouri Commission—or virtually all of the more than $300 million it spends annually in Missouri maintaining and upgrading its network. (I cite these estimates in my affidavit *In the Matter of AT&T Communications of the Southwest, Inc.'s Petition for Arbitration* and the corresponding *Petition of MCI Telecommunications*, Cases No. TO-97-40 and TO-97-67, before the Public Service Commission of the State of Missouri, Aug. 14, 1997. The corresponding estimates by Southwestern Bell for Texas, a loss of $1.36 billion revenues annually [that would be produced, under the same assumption, by the recommendations of AT&T] and $3.8 billion annual expenditures on the network, are cited in my affidavit before the Texas Commission, PUC Docket Nos. 16189 et al., Sept. 15, 1997. While I was not in a position to endorse these estimates, I found them plausible on the basis of my understanding of the bases of the rates proposed, in the one case by the commission, in the other by AT&T.

B. Their Asserted Barrier to Entry

Criticisms of inflated access charges are frequently accompanied by the assertion or implication—plausible but flatly incorrect—that the high charges for access constitute direct barriers to the entry of competitors.[155] These assertions either ignore or fail to comprehend that the ability of rival companies to compete with the local telephone companies, while paying them charges for access far above the cost of providing it, is determined not by the absolute level of those charges but by the *margin* between them and the prices that the incumbent telephone companies charge for their own competitive retail services.[156]

---

[155] See, e.g., Mayo, Crew, Economides, Hubbard, Kleindorfer and Martins-Filho, *op. cit.*, filed in a number of state arbitration proceedings involving the terms of access by competitors to facilities owned by incumbent local exchange companies, asserting that charges above TSLRIC for network elements (the same reasoning would apply to carrier access charges) constitutes a barrier to entry in the form of an entry tax—"an extra cost that entrants have to pay to enter." (pp. 16-17) Similarly, a letter to Chairman Hundt of the FCC by five former chief economists of the Antitrust Division of the U.S. Department of Justice, dated Dec. 2, 1996, asserts that such charges "tend ... to sustain local monopolies," because "competing providers might have to pay more than a competitive price for necessary inputs ..."

[156] The larger the mark-up above cost included in the carrier access charge, however, the smaller the total size of the market, because of the elasticity of demand. For this reason, an absolutely higher access charge would leave less room in the market for firms of minimally efficient size than a smaller mark-up, and in this sense constitute a barrier to entry. For this reason, if the requisite subsidy is to be raised through these charges, the size of the mark-up must of course be subject to strict regulatory determination that it be no greater than necessary to enable companies to recover their total legitimated costs.

John Haring has provided a particularly vigorous exposition of that deleterious effect of inflated access charges. He observes that the more rapid *growth* in the long-distance market during the transition to a more efficient price structure induced by their reduction would be additionally simulative of competitive entry; and that this in turn would exert pressures on utility commissions to correct their current inefficient pricing structures (an observation almost identical to one I made more than 25 years ago about the effect of "cream-skimming" entry in my *The Economics of Regulation*, Vol. II, pp. 221-23). Finally, he contends, even if the reduction in access charges (with ILECs tempted not to reduce their retail prices fully correspondingly) were to encourage the entry of productively less efficient rivals, that

(*continued...*)

Essential to the conception of an entry barrier is that it confer on incumbents a competitive *advantage* over would-be rivals. As Professor George J. Stigler put it:

> a barrier to entry may be defined as a cost of producing ... which must be borne by a firm which seeks to enter an industry but is not borne by firms already in the industry.[157]

The markups above incremental cost in the charges to competitors for network access (or for network elements) would confer no such advantage. Far from imposing a cost on would-be rivals that would not be borne by the incumbents, permitting the latter to recover embedded and ongoing costs associated with their unique service obligations in this way would preserve or *restore* a competitive parity to a situation in which it is the incumbents that have incurred and/or continue to incur costs *that are or have not been borne by their challengers.*[158] Incorporation of a mark-up in access charges to long-distance carriers (or charges to CLECs for unbundled elements) equivalent to the mark-up incorporated in the corresponding retail rates of the ILECs is not just *compatible* with efficient competition in the affected retail markets but *necessary* to ensure it is efficient.

(...*continued*)

> would probably be a small price to pay for (1) the consequent undeniable improvement in allocative efficiency that reduced long-distance rates would entail and (2) the more powerful pressures that such entry would exert for improvements in productive efficiency by all parties. "Can local telecommunications be self-policing?" *Telecommunications Policy,* Vol. 19 (1995), pp. 91-104. In the presence of an unwillingness of regulatory commissions to engage in the rebalancing of inefficient rate structures (about the necessity for which Haring and I emphatically agree), however, it seems irrational to suggest that they deliberately invite possibly productively inefficient entry in order to put pressure on themselves to correct those irrational structures.

[157] *The Organization of Industry,* Homewood: Richard D. Irwin, 1968, p. 67. See the fuller discussion in W. Kip Viscusi, John M. Vernon and Joseph E. Harrington, Jr., *Economics of Regulation and Antitrust,* 2d ed., Cambridge: The MIT Press, 1995, pp. 158-62.

[158] The burden imposed on the incumbents by the two kinds of costs differ in the fundamental respect that only the ongoing costs have to be recovered if the companies

(*continued...*)

The FCC's clear recognition of this fact in its May 1997 *Access Charge Reform First Report and Order* (par. 275), as well as its expression of opinion that protections against anti-competitive squeezes are sufficient (par. 278-82), makes a welcome contrast with its erroneous opposite assertions—in the face of frequent reminders that "It's the margin, stupid!" [159]—in its preceding *Interconnection Order*. Since regulatory commissions routinely require the telephone companies to set their own retail prices high enough to recover the same charges as they impose on their competitors for use of their facilities—and the Telecommunications Act explicitly requires this "imputation" of carrier access charges—the frequent assertions by interested parties that the inflated access charges are "anti-competitive"[160] are simply wrong.[161]

(*...continued*)

are to continue in operation in the long run. As we have already observed, however, so long as the companies continue to feel an obligation to their stockholders to try to recover costs to which they regard them as entitled by historical regulatory practices, they will tend—so long as competition is less than pure or perfect (that is, so long as they retain any monopoly power by those standards)—to hold prices above incremental costs, even though at the expense of loss of market share to equally or even less efficient rivals, in order to maximize their recovery of those sunk costs. Of course, so would any profit-maximizing seller with such monopoly power, *regardless* of whether or to what extent it could rationalize that behavior in terms of recovering sunk costs to which it believes itself entitled. The question for public policy, however, is whether the allocative inefficiency and other harmful consequences expounded by John Haring (note 156, above) flowing from regulators permitting recovery of these sunk costs in markups of charges for access or unbundled network elements is justified by the obligation to permit utility companies recovery of such sunk costs. To the extent it is, the Efficient Component Pricing Rule would provide full protection for equally efficient entrants.

[159] See, for example, the transcript of the FCC Panel Discussion Forum, *Economics of Interconnection*, May 21, 1996, p. 132 and the Declaration by Timothy J. Tardiff and me, in CC Docket No. 96-98, *In the Matter of Implementation of the Local Competition Provision in the Telecommunications Act of 1996*, May 30, 1996, pp. 11-13.

[160] See note 155, above.

[161] See the qualifications in note 156, above. Franklin M. Fisher has pointed out that, contrary to the assertions of some defenders of the ECPR, it does not preclude the possibility of some business being taken over or retained by a less-efficient incumbent. His argument does not, I think, deny the proposition that if the ILEC is prohibited from reducing its rates for competitive services below the access charges

(*continued...*)

In view of the FCC's dismissal of the complaints by the IXCs that current access charges generate monopoly profits and its rejection of proposals that they be promptly reduced to incremental costs, on the ground, among others, that it had first to determine whether the LECs should be compensated for their sunk costs there or in some other way (*Access Charge Reform First Report and Order*, pars. 45-46, 49), it cannot but be disappointing that the Commission merely states its intention to issue a separate order that

---

(*...continued*)

plus its own incremental costs of performing the contested operations (as the ECPR requires), it cannot succeed in squeezing out equally efficient competitors. What he observes, however, is that if—as seems likely—both competitors and incumbents find (or believe) they can profit-maximize with rates *above* their own incremental costs, the fact that the incremental *cost* of access to the incumbent firm is lower than the access *charges* that its competitors may pay could dictate lower retail prices by the former than the latter and the possibility, therefore, of the ILEC taking over some business even though its own incremental *supply* costs are no lower or might even be higher than those of its rivals. "An Analysis of Switched Access Pricing and the Telecommunications Act of 1996," Attachment 1, MCI Reply Comments, CC Docket No. 96-98, May 30, 1996.

It is difficult to understand, however, why the ILECs would, perversely, insist on supplying a large portion of their sales with their own facilities, if their incremental costs were higher than those of the incumbents, in view of the ubiquitous arrangements under which ILECs generally and RBOCs specifically resell the long-distance services of incumbent long-distance carriers—at rates reportedly in the one-to-two-cents-per-minute range—because of the very large excess capacity in the present long-distance networks, on the one side, and the large volume of purchases to which the incumbents have been able to commit themselves, on the other. "NYNEX to Resell Sprint Service," Bloomberg LLP, April 24, 1996; "Bells, GTE Lay Out Marketing Strategies, Swap Success Stories at New York Conference," *Telecommunications Reports*, Sept. 26, 1996; McElroy, C., "BellSouth To Buy Time On AT&T's Long-Distance Network," Bloomberg LLP, June 19, 1996. Moreover, against the theoretically possible source of inefficiency identified by Professor Fisher, if the RBOCs were permitted to offer interLATA service, would have to be weighed the improvement in both allocative and productive efficiency in the latter markets flowing from the intensified competition their entry would precipitate. See, e.g., Richard Schmalensee, William Taylor, J. Douglas Zona, Paul Hinton, "An Analysis of the Welfare Effects of Long Distance Market Entry by an Integrated Access and Long Distance Provider," National Economic Research Associates, Inc., discussion paper, 1997. Moreover, that intensified competitiveness, consequent on the entry of the RBOCs, which MCI used the Fisher exposition to oppose, would mitigate the essential condition of the adverse effect predicted by him—the ability of firms to profit-maximize by holding rates substantially above incremental costs.

will ... address 'historical cost' recovery: whether and to what extent carriers should receive compensation for the recovery of the allocated costs of past investments if competitive market conditions prevent them from recovering such costs in their charges for interstate access services (par. 14),

for two related reasons. First, it postpones the full reduction in those highly inefficient charges to efficient levels. Second, it perpetuates the uncertainty, already generated by the interconnection orders, about the extent to which the carriers will, indeed, be permitted to recover those costs. The way to move promptly to a competitive regime is to resolve the huge transitional problem of stranded costs one way or another and make prompt provision for the recovery of whatever amounts are settled on.[162]

C. Should the markup on Access be Reduced in Reflection of Anticipated Net Revenues from Overpriced Services?

The MCI Comments in the access reform proceedings suggest that the size of the markup in the access charge should be reduced to take into account the net revenues that the LECs may reasonably be expected to earn from such other offerings as vertical, video and, eventually, interLATA services (pp. 3-5).

---

[162] The equivocal position of the FCC on this issue contrasts with the forthright declaration of intention by the Federal Energy Regulatory Commission, in its decision to permit the recovery of "legitimate, prudent and verifiable stranded costs" with mark-ups in transmission charges, while also, under instructions of the Energy Policy Act of 1992, requiring electric utility companies to wheel independently generated power for wholesale sales. *Promoting Wholesale Competition Through Open Access Non-discriminatory Services by Public Utilities and Recovery of Stranded Costs by Public Utilities and Transmitting Utilities*, Docket Nos. RM95-8-000 and RM94-7-001, *Order No. 888, Final Rule*, issued April 24, 1996. All the states that have enacted deregulation laws involving the electric power industry, except New Hampshire, similarly explicitly allow the utility companies "to recover substantially all of their so-called stranded costs" through such devices as markups in the charges for use of their distribution facilities or "exit fees" levied directly on departing customers." "Electric-Deregulation Machine Starts to Pick Up Steam," *The Wall Street Journal*, July 14, 1997, p. B4.

The last of these suggestions is particularly incongruous—indeed, outrageously self-serving. It would clearly be inconsistent with efficient competition in the *unregulated* markets—specifically, it would handicap the LECs in that competition—if they alone had to continue to charge rates above competitive levels for those offerings because regulation was requiring them to rely on those contributions to recover the legitimate costs of regulated operations. [163] It would strongly tempt them to hold a price umbrella over their competitors—such as MCI—in intraLATA and local markets, so long as they continued to have the major share of that business.

More broadly, MCI's suggestion conflicts with our national policy to subject the offer of the contribution-generating services to competition. Continued regulation of basic rates that assumes a continued generation of subsidy from these other services would frustrate that intention. More compellingly, the steps we have already taken to effectuate that national policy have made its continued generation *impossible*. So long as competitors can now assemble the network elements necessary to provide such currently overpriced services *at cost*—let alone the TSLRIC-BS version that MCI has consistently advocated—those inflated prices cannot survive.[164]

What the Commission seems to have inadequately recognized is that the same reluctance it properly exhibits about prescribing a quick reduction in carrier access charges to incremental costs, in recognition of their continued necessary contribution to the subsidy (and recovery of sunk costs) until some alternative source is found—or rates rebalanced—logically

---

[163] On the differing nature of that compulsion with respect to sunk costs and the *ongoing* regulatorily imposed costs of fulfilling their unique public utility obligations—in particular, the costs of the underpricing of residential services—see note 158, above.

[164] See Haring and Rohlfs, *op. cit.*, note 20, above, pp. 8-11. To offer just a single example, the Minnesota Public Utilities Commission set a rate for unbundled loops in Minneapolis in 1997 at $12 per month. With residential flat rate service in that city at $18.50 (including the $3.50 subscriber line charge) and similar basic service to business at $45, not surprisingly MCI promptly began offering business service, at a $38 rate, planning to provide it with U S West loops.

applies equally, in principle, to the prices it set for network elements; to the statute's disallowance of any mark-ups above incremental costs in charges for interconnection with ILECs for terminating *local* calls, without regard to whether the CLEC assumes similar public service obligations;[165] and to its dictation of ample wholesale discounts to resellers of local services *whose retail rates are already below incremental cost.* Just as the access charges, both intra- and interstate, have been a means of continuing the necessary flow of contribution from long-distance services, so have the overpricing at the state level of vertical services and of dialtone to businesses, particularly in concentrated metropolitan areas. These are similarly threatened with undermining if CLECs are enabled, by being permitted to interconnect with ILECs either at cost or on a bill-and-keep or symmetrical reciprocal compensation basis, or to purchase basic residential dialtone service from the incumbents at their regulatorily suppressed retail prices *less* the prescribed wholesale discounts, giving them a free ticket of admission to the markets for the overpriced services at the expense of the incumbents.[166] (Section 251 (C) (4) (B) of

---

[165] The Act prescribes "terms … for the mutual and reciprocal recovery by each carrier of [such] costs ... on the basis of...the additional costs of terminating such calls." Sec. 252 (d)(2)(A)(i-ii).

[166] See my spelling out of this problem in my "A Free Ticket to Rich Telecom Markets," *The Wall Street Journal,* Nov. 10, 1995, p. A-15, evaluating the demand of AT&T for large wholesale discounts:

> what AT&T is demanding is an equal shot at the overpriced markets without having to bear any of the costs that justify that overpricing.

The same criticism may properly be directed at Professors Kaserman's and Mayo's proposed efficient wholesale price as the retail price less avoidable costs (their approval of the FCC's TSLRIC-based definition of which I have already observed and criticized in Section III.C.2., above) even for services whose retail prices are suppressed by regulation below cost. For example, they posit a TSLRIC of $7 per unit at the wholesale and $5 at the retail level and a regulated retail price not of $12 but $10, to which they would apply the same $5 TSLRIC of retailing, to yield a wholesale price of $5. Such a wholesale price, preserving a retail margin of $5 for resellers, they assert, would neither encourage inefficient nor discourage efficient entry into retailing. *Op. cit.,* pp. 101-02.

The latter inference, drawn from the $5 margin on the resold services, is incorrect. The Kaserman/Mayo recommendation would distort the competition between the CLECs and the ILECs, by protecting the former from the burden of the subsidy.

(continued...)

the Act recognizes the danger that rate structures embodying cross-sub-sidization could be undermined by its sales for resale provisions by per-mitting state Commissions to prohibit resales of subsidized services, acquired in this way, to customers not entitled to the subsidies. But nei-ther it nor the Commission has authorized states to prohibit the cream-skimming that occurs when CLECs are enabled by the FCC's own rules to acquire unbundled inputs—e.g., loops—at TELRIC-approximating costs and using them to cream-skim business subscribers' rates.)

The point of these mark-ups, it is worth re-emphasizing, is not merely to afford the ILECs an opportunity to recover their total costs and to con-tinue the regulatorily-prescribed cross-subsidization. It is also, by im-posing on their challengers the same proportionate burdens as they have themselves been forced by regulation to bear, to eliminate the invitation to inefficient competition in the provision of the overpriced services ex-tended by the present distorted rate structures.

(...*continued*)

They would have available to them the $5 per unit cost of efficient retailing, while forcing the incumbents to bear it by selling at a $5 wholesale price services that cost them $7. The result would be to give resellers (such as AT&T) direct access to the market for the overpriced services, in direct competition with the ILECs, with-out having to pay the $2 per unit "ticket of admission to rich telecom markets."

I should point out, in fairness, that Kaserman and Mayo are fully aware of the in-efficiencies entailed in the underpricing of some of the latter services and have consistently recommended the financing of such subsidies in other, competitively neutral ways. The fact remains that their exposition here ignores what makes it possible for the incumbent LECs to incur the loss that they posit on basic residen-tial services. Obviously, it is the offsetting, inefficiently large, regulatorily man-dated mark-ups on the other services, to which markets their proposed discount to resellers of the basic services would give them free access, without having to bear the burden of the subsidy.

In effect, their proposal—the same as has been consistently made by AT&T— would permit CLECs (like AT&T) to play the game of heads-we-win, tails-you-lose—availing themselves of the right to purchase unbundled network elements at bare TSLRIC-BS and using those inputs to undercut the hapless ILECs in offering the *overpriced* services (as in the example cited in note 164, above) and having re-course to the FCC's generous wholesale pricing rules in order to purchase *under-priced* services at the subsidized level.

In negotiations with ILECs and in arbitration proceedings, AT&T has demanded that the incumbents deliver to it at TSLRIC-BS all the network elements—the "platform"—necessary to serve a particular customer. This demand raises two obvious questions: How does it differ from a demand for the ability simply to resell the retail services, under the resale requirement of the Act, and what kind of "competition" would this constitute? Moreover, observe the ability this would give AT&T or any other CLEC to work both sides of the unbalanced rate structure street. It could use the "platform," at bare costs—however defined—as the means of supplying the overpriced, cross-subsidizing services, while demanding the full, prescribed wholesale discount from the suppressed retail prices of the subsidized services.

It was precisely on the ground that

> to permit such an acquisition of already combined elements [i.e., a "platform"] at cost based rates for unbundled access would obliterate the careful distinctions Congress has drawn ... between access to unbundled network elements on the one hand and the purchase at wholesale rates of an incumbent's telecommunications retail services for resale on the other

that the Circuit Court of Appeals voided the FCC's rules requiring ILECs to comply with the former demand.[167]

A former state commission chairman has protested the contrast between the FCC's concern about interfering with the subsidies from both interstate and intrastate carrier access services and the threat posed by the

---

[167] *Iowa Utilities Board, et al, v. FCC* (see note 16, above) *Order on Petitions for Rehearing*, Oct. 14, 1997. AT&T has consistently contended, in one forum or another, that it simply cannot afford to enter into the competitive offer of local services unless it receives discounts on the order of one-half of the local rates, whether explicitly on its purchases of retail services from the ILECs for resale or in rates for the "platform" it demands at its low TELRIC-BS estimates. If these contentions are justified, perhaps the only proper inference is that genuine, ubiquitous competition in the local residential market is a will-of-the-wisp, so long as we insist on a set of regulatory policies that is fundamentally inconsistent with it. See V.B., below, "The Case for Doing the Right Thing," and VII.

provisions in its interconnection order relating to the subsidies relied upon at the state level from services other than access:

> What the Commission seems to ignore is that State regulators also consciously use subsidy mechanisms in services other than switched access, such as vertical services, which are defined as network elements as well as telecommunications services under the Commission's rules. Strictly in terms of access, the Commission speaks of its "desire to err on the side of caution where universal service may be implicated" (see Order, par. 719), but it expressly prohibits the states from acting on similar desires in terms of the State's non-access related subsidies.[168]

There is simply no longer any escaping the inevitability of reforming our system for ensuring a continued close to universal subscription to telephone service, as well as living up to the regulatory bargain with the incumbent telephone companies. The present method, relying on markups on toll, carrier access and a host of "intrastate" services alike, is both grossly inefficient[169] and unsustainable under our new national policies. The best method by far would be simply to get—or let competition get—those various rates right, with direct subsidies of the charges for basic service to impecunious subscribers. Since, however, Congress has in its wisdom called instead for continued universal underpricing of those services—financed in "competitively neutral" ways—I turn first to that fourth or fifth best alternative.

---

[168] Affidavit of Kenneth Gordon, In Support of Florida Public Service Commission Appeal of FCC First Report and Order in CC Docket No. 96-98, Sept. 12, 1996, p. 4, note 7.

[169] Since the demand for vertical services and second lines—upon which, among others, the states rely as sources of subsidy—is clearly more elastic than for basic service, continued reliance on them for this purpose perpetuates the inefficiencies of the historical price structure. Assertions by interested parties such as MCI that (a) economic efficiency calls for a reduction in carrier access charges (which it does) and (b) that such reductions will be consistent with giving the LECs a fair shot at recovering their costs because they can continue to expect to derive contributions from these other services are simply logically inconsistent. Indeed, it seems fair to characterize them as cynical—seeking as they do to capitalize on the political attractiveness of giving consumers some visible benefits from the Telecommunications Act, for which it could claim credit, by altering the terms of the regulatory bargain with the utility companies, at the expense of their shareholders.

V. The False Promise of a "Competitively Neutrally-Financed" Universal Service Fund

The many deficiencies of the "reforms" already adopted and now proposed—the TELRIC-BS basis for pricing unbundled network elements, the postponement of a decision about the dimension of the ILECs' entitlement to recovery of their sunk costs, the failure to recognize the legitimacy in the interim of mark-ups above incremental costs in charges for interconnection with ILECs for terminating *local* calls, and the dictation of ample wholesale discounts to resellers of local services whose retail rates are already below incremental cost—can all in principle be ameliorated (but, as I will point out, not—by a long shot—wholly remedied, even in principle) by the alternative method of financing "universal service" called for by the Telecommunications Act. That is to say, these revenue deficiencies and cross-subsidies can be made good or financed in a manner that, while still falling far short of economically efficient, would nevertheless be less distorting of competition than the present system of bypass-inducing markups in the charges by the incumbent telephone companies alone. Such a fund, financed by equiproportionate levies on all customers' bills or on all service providers and distributed (a) solely to the ILECs, to the extent necessary to compensate them for their unique sunk costs and (b) to all providers in proportion as they assume the obligation of providing the services that are to be subsidized, could not only satisfy the revenue entitlements of the incumbent companies but make possible competition in areas where the present regulated rates, falling in varying degrees below efficient levels, preclude it.

The independently financed Universal Service Fund is, therefore, the necessary third leg of the stool of the policies the Act prescribes for opening the industry to competition. The three legs have to be of the same length. If (a) basic residential and rural services (and now service to schools, libraries and regional health facilities) are to continue to be priced below economically efficient levels, (b) the services that have historically provided the requisite subsidy are to be subjected increasingly to competition, and (c) the local telephone companies responsible for providing that basic service ubiquitously are no longer going to be able to raise the necessary funds by charging long-distance carriers and local competitors rates for access, interconnection or for unbundled network elements sufficiently above incremental costs, then it becomes necessary to find some other source of financing that, by making all competitive suppliers subject to the same proportionate burdens, would permit the funds to be raised even in the face of competition and, at the same time, prevent that burden of the ILECs encouraging inefficient competitive entry.

That is the theory and it is appealing.

Its application is certain to be a good deal more messy.
First, it is unlikely to be any easier politically to impose an explicit tax on all bills for telecommunications services than it would be to do the economically right thing in the first place: simply raise the basic residential and other subsidized charges and reduce—or permit competition to reduce—all the others that currently subsidize them.

What we are witnessing, therefore, is a transfer of the forum of arguments about the size of the LECs' revenue entitlements from the access charge to the several USF proceedings. There, it may safely be predicted, the political pressures that continue to suppress prices of the subsidized services will continue to discourage the levy of "competitively neutral" and minimally inefficient taxes sufficient to fill the gap. If we now recognize that added to those historical political pressures is the pressure on commissions quickly to show some positive benefits to consumers from the new Act, we must recognize the danger—indeed, the likelihood—that they will be more forceful in reducing the one than in increasing the other.

It is both significant and troublesome, therefore, that after the FCC had promulgated its proposed rules with respect to the pricing of unbundled network elements and of retail services for resale and carrier access, it postponed completion of the promised third leg of the stool for at least 18 months.[170]

---

[170] In its *Report and Order In the Matter of Federal-State Joint Board on Universal Service*, CC Docket No. 96-45, adopted May 7, 1997 (hereinafter, *Universal Service*
(continued...)

This delay by no means necessarily reflects adversely on the Commission. The tasks imposed upon it by the Telecommunications Act were gargantuan. In particular, the task of developing, under intense political pressure and public scrutiny, a rational, comprehensive system for defining, maintaining and financing all of the subsidies that public policy continues to insist on providing for basic residential rates generally and insists now on extending to schools, libraries and health facilities—all henceforward to be financed "rationally" instead of by the present crazy-quilt of internal subsidies—was in essential respects oxymoronic. In assessing the FCC's performance, it is necessary to bear in mind as well the fact that its own direct authority extends only to methods of recovering the costs allocated to the federal level—25 percent of the cost of loops, for example—with the major portion of the responsibility residing with the states. Moreover—even though I will have criticisms to make of what it did—fairness requires acknowledgment that the Commission did take some important steps, in its *Access Reform Order* of the same date, in the direction of rationalizing that major system of internal subsidization at the federal level.

At the same time, the Commission has only itself to blame for having presumed to stipulate the results of what the Act clearly envisioned was to have been a process of direct negotiations between ILECs and would-be CLECs, supplemented by arbitration and subject to confirmation or resolution by the state commissions, as the Circuit Court of Appeals held in staying the FCC's *Interconnection Order*.

Moreover, there are troubling signs that when and if a reform system for subsidizing universality of subscription is ever provided, it will have been subjected to all sorts of pressures to whittle it away—both quantitatively

---

(...*continued*)

   Order), the Commission announced its intention to "establish a forward-looking universal service support mechanism based on forward-looking economic costs for non-rural carriers" to take effect on Jan. 1, 1999 (par. 26), with the revision of the methods of support for rural carriers, including exploration of the possible use of competitive bidding as a means of determining the requisite subsidies, postponed beyond that date.

(that is, in fixing its requisite size) and in terms of the competitive neutrality and efficient pricing that it was intended to ensure. Moreover, as I will explain in Part VI., below, the access charge reforms already announced by the Commission betray a deplorable propensity to boast publicly about benefits while concealing costs, at some substantial sacrifice of efficiency.

There are two troubling signs, in particular, that are directly pertinent in the present context. The first is the FCC's proposed measure of the cost of providing the basic service in question, the difference between which and regulated rates would be the measure of the requisite subsidy. The second is the measure of revenues that would be credited against those estimated costs to determine the residual subsidy.

A. The Dimensions of the Universal Funding Requirement

1. The competitive benchmark

Suppose society chose to subsidize a particular service that it hoped would be supplied competitively if the combination of regulated price and subsidy were right. The first measure required would be the amount by which the price necessary to elicit the desired supply in an unsubsidized market exceeded the price society was prepared to see charged consumers directly. That price would have to cover incremental costs. In addition, it would, in the presence of large economies of scale and scope, have to incorporate markups contributing to the recovery of total economic—i.e., current and forward-looking—costs. Moreover, as I have already expounded the case, it would incorporate an additional markup for the recovery of sunk costs of the incumbent supplier. As is also widely understood, finally, if those various markups were to be efficient —i.e., were to minimize the inefficiencies consequent on the necessity to set prices above marginal cost—they would as a general proposition vary inversely with the elasticities of the demands for the several services. Failure of the Commission to incorporate in its calculation of the required explicit subsidy for "universal service" a markup reflecting the relative inelasticity of demand for that service[171]—would necessitate an inefficiently *large* markup on the other, for the most part more price-elastic services.[172]

Not surprisingly, in light of its earlier decision about the pricing of unbundled network elements, the Commission proposes to determine the costs to be recovered from the combination of regulated prices and subsidy as the purely

> forward-looking economic cost of constructing and operating the network facilities and functions used to provide the supported services .... the costs that would be incurred by an efficient carrier in the market (*Universal Service Order*, par. 224),

defined over

> a period long enough that all costs may be treated as variable and avoidable (par. 250),

with the same qualification as it adopted for network elements, that the models estimating that cost

> must include the ILECs' wire centers as the center of the loop network and the outside plant should terminate at ILECs' current wire centers. (par. 250)

Evidently in the belief that this last qualification eliminates the unusual

---

[171] So the Massachusetts Department of Public Utilities, in directing the New England Telephone Company to file "an illustrative tariff," instructed it "that, in the illustrative tariffs, any residual revenue requirement remaining after rates were set at marginal cost was to be collected in a customer charge or other similar non-elastic price element." D.P.U. 89-300 at p. 17, June 1990.

[172] The notion of incorporating in the *subsidy* for basic residential telephone service a markup properly reflective of the relative inelasticity of its demand, in a situation in which it is clear that the markup is to be collected not in the price of that service but instead from services with more elastic demands, sounds like an exercise in futility. Indeed it is, in essential respects. But conceivably the requisite taxes could be levied in a manner less inefficient—and the expectation clearly is that it will be levied in a manner more consistent with competitive neutrality—than the present burdens of internal subsidization.

risks (described in III.C., above) that an entrant would incur in building an entire system from scratch, it specifies that for non-rural carriers

> [t]he rate of return must be either the authorized federal rate of re-
> turn on interstate services, currently 11.25 percent, or the state's
> prescribed rate of return for intrastate services .... Economic lives
> and future net salvage percentages used in calculating depreciation
> expense must be within the FCC-authorized range. (par. 250)

The Commission's justification for requiring the use of these hypothetical incremental costs rather than those of the incumbent LECs (which it
refers to, loosely, as an "embedded cost" measure[173]), while familiar
from our discussion of the same choice as it applied to the pricing of unbundled network elements, is worth reproducing because it expands
upon the FCC's previous rationalization:

> to the extent that it differs from forward-looking economic cost,
> embedded cost provides the wrong signals to potential entrants and
> existing carriers. The use of embedded cost would *discourage pru-*
> *dent investment planning* because carriers could receive support for
> inefficient as well as efficient investments. The Joint Board ex-
> plained that when 'embedded costs are above forward-looking
> costs, support of embedded costs would *direct* carriers to make in-
> efficient investments that may not be financially viable when there
> is competitive entry.' The Joint Board also explained that if embed-
> ded cost is below forward-looking economic cost, support based on
> embedded costs would erect an entry barrier to new competitors,
> because revenue per customer and support, together, would be less
> than the forward-looking economic cost of providing the supported
> services. We agree ... We also agree ... that the use of embedded
> cost to calculate universal service support would lead to subsidiza-
> tion of inefficient carriers at the expense of efficient carriers and
> could *create disincentives for carriers to operate efficiently.* (par.
> 228, stress supplied, footnote references omitted)

---

[173] See note 129, above.

It is, of course, difficult to quarrel with the proposition that it is undesirable to subsidize or encourage inefficiency. I maintain, however, that, just as in the case of the pricing of network elements, the proper basis for the subsidy would be the actual incremental costs of the incumbent LECs rather than the blank slate version endorsed by the Joint Board and adopted by the FCC.

Suppose, to take the second situation they hypothesize (and clearly regard as the less likely), the first basis (which they label imprecisely, "embedded costs") is lower than the cost that would be incurred by the hypothetical efficient entrant. In that event, the combination of price and subsidy based on the second, higher level of incremental costs adopted by the FCC would obviously encourage inefficient entry. The Commission is not writing on a blank slate. The ILECs already have ubiquitous networks serving their entire franchise territories and are constantly providing service to new customers within them. If the incremental cost of their doing so were lower than TSLRIC-BS, the combined price and subsidy calculated on the latter basis would give the incumbent a larger subsidy than it actually required to recover its economic costs and offer even less-efficient potential rivals an opportunity to challenge it successfully. If potential entrants require a subsidy greater than would be dictated by the actual LRIC of incumbents, their entry would be inefficient.

If instead the hypothetical TSLRIC were *lower* than the ILEC's actual incremental costs, the subsidy would be inadequate to enable the utility company to recover those costs. Not only would this make it unwilling to extend service and violate such entitlement as it has to recover its costs not imprudently incurred; it would be inadequate also to give competitors the *full inducement*—such as they would have in a competitive market—that prices plus subsidies based on the incumbent's cost would offer them to displace it.

It is clearly the latter situation that the Commission has in mind when it rejects the "embedded cost" method on the ground that it would reward and encourage inefficiency on the part of both incumbents and challengers. The proper remedies in that case, however, are the ones that the Commission itself has given in its *Access Charge Reform* decision (see Part III.C.3., above). The cure for inadequate incentives on the part of incumbents or challengers to maximize efficiency is (1) rate caps for both prices and proffered subsidies, indexed for inflation and achievable improvements in productivity (once their future course is divorced from the actual costs of the companies, suppliers have every incentive to maximize efficiency), and (2) facilities-based competition itself, which the Commission's proffered basis for subsidy would tend to discourage and subsidy levels calculated on the basis of the incremental costs of the *incumbent* companies would properly encourage.

The Commission's notion, in any event, that subsidies set high enough to cover the costs of inefficiencies in the operations of the ILECs would "discourage prudent investment planning" and "create disincentives for carriers to operate efficiently" is more wrong than right. While it is difficult to deny the likelihood that the more generous the subsidies, the less intensely suppliers are likely to be motivated to minimize their costs, the fact remains that once the subsidies and their future course are fixed, remediable or avoidable inefficiencies come directly out of profits. While entrants that can serve the market at incremental costs lower than those of the incumbent might, under duopolistic or oligopolistic competition, be tempted not to undercut the latter's price, preferring instead to retain the difference in costs, the way in which they can obtain and retain those potential profits is still to provide the services as efficiently as possible.

The likely consequence of the Commission's choice of competitive benchmark costs, already painfully visible in negotiations for use of unbundled ILEC network elements, will be intensely contested trials-by-models, in which competitors of the ILECs with little intention of providing basic residential service ubiquitously with their own facilities have every incentive to come in with low estimates of the true costs of doing so and, therefore, of the size of the necessary fund (and also arguing strenuously against using those funds to pay off the incumbents' sunk costs), and the LECs under correspondingly strong incentives to exaggerate those costs—an unequal contest, since the referee will have a strong incentive to minimize the tax.[174]

---

[174] There is one essential function of the fund for which the use of such "proxy cost models" will be essential, however. In determining the size of the subsidy to be

(continued...)

2. The treatment of complementary revenues

The second source of concern is the Commission's decision that the size of the subsidy be reduced in reflection of the net earnings or contribution that providers of the basic service would be expected to obtain from vertical or other overpriced services[175]. The reader will recognize here a variant of the illogical argument (see Part III.A.3., above) to the effect that *basic residential service* is not really cross-subsidized because, assertedly, residential *subscribers*—either in the aggregate or in large sections of the country—produce *total revenues* that fully recover the total cost of serving them.

The suggestion has additional plausibility when it is made in the context of determining the size of the subsidy necessary to induce competitors to enter upon the offer of basic telephone service. Clearly their entry decision will be determined by the total revenues that they may expect to obtain by that entry compared with the total costs of providing all the services they expect to sell, rather than by the charge for dial tone alone. The answers to this plausible suggestion flow from the ones we have already given. The first is that since consumers will purchase these various services—dialtone, vertical services, toll and the rest—in varying proportions, efficiency requires that each be priced at its efficient level. It is precisely the failure of present price structures to respect this principle that

---

(...continued)

offered equally to the incumbent LECs and their challengers, to the extent the latter assume corresponding burdens, it will be essential to recognize that the costs of serving customers vary widely, particularly from one geographic location to another. In principle, the per-customer subsidies should vary with the difference between the cost of serving each one of them and the regulatorily mandated rates. In practice, it will be necessary to estimate those cost differences by geographic areas, with their several estimated costs refined down to the smallest practicable area, sufficiently uniform in cost characteristics that the carriers serving the higher-cost customers within each are not unduly disadvantaged. This will be so regardless of whether the object of the inquiry is an estimate of the cost to the incumbent LEC of serving these various groups of customers or the costs that would be confronted by a hypothetical new entrant.

[175] Under its scheme, the subsidy would be determined by subtracting from the estimated costs of providing the supported services "a nationwide revenue benchmark calculated on the basis of average revenue per line." (par. 223)

produces multi-billion dollar annual welfare losses, *even though* telephone companies in the aggregate presumably recover their total costs.

The second answer is closely related. As the Commission explicitly recognizes, to its credit, the competition that it is our national policy to encourage makes the overpricing of the subsidizing services unsustainable.[176] Moreover, the way in which the Telecommunications Act and the FCC's interpretation of it has proceeded to make those cross-subsidies unsustainable ensures that competitors will not enter into the local markets *on a facilities basis* unless the subsidies are sufficient to make up the difference between the suppressed rates and the incremental costs (or efficient prices) of providing *basic service* itself. If they are not, CLECs will purchase the requisite underpriced basic services from the incumbents at Commission-prescribed wholesale discounts sufficient to recover the costs of the retailing function—leaving it to the ILECs to bear the full costs of that underpricing—and thereby obtain free access to the market for the overpriced complementary services. Alternatively, they will purchase the requisite inputs from the incumbents at TELRIC-BS-based rates and use them to undercut the ILECs' rates for those lucrative services. If competition is, indeed, to be effective in all potentially competitive markets and for all services, their several prices must individually recover at least their several incremental costs. Both efficiency and competition will tolerate no other outcome.

---

[176]   We believe that, as competition develops, the marketplace itself will identify intrastate implicit universal service support, and the states will be compelled by those marketplace forces to move that support to explicit sustainable mechanisms ...

      —i.e., from overpricing subsidizing services to explicit, competitively-neutrally financed subsidies. (*Universal Service Order*, par. 14; see also par. 17.)

    The gradual erosion of the subsidies incorporated in present prices, under pressure of competition, might, serendipitously, have the same effect as the indexation of the proffered subsidies for inflation and achievable improvements in productivity that I have already advocated. It seems more logical, however, and, one would hope, more productive of accurate results, to rely on unbiased direct estimation than on serendipity.

B. The Case for Doing the Right Thing

In these circumstances, people who do not have to run for public office owe it to themselves, at the very least, to reiterate that a full rebalancing of rates to economically efficient levels, along with targeted subsidized rates for low-income families (and such institutional users as we decide to subsidize), would be a far preferable way of ensuring continued universality of subscription to telephone service. After all:

- We do not generally try to make what we regard as essential parts of a decent standard of living universally available by holding their prices to all purchasers below costs. We do not do it for food, medical services or home heating fuels. Apart from rent controls in some localities, to the extent we do it for housing, we do it by direct subsidy to only those people who might otherwise be unable to afford it.

- The ideal way of paying for such social programs, including the Act's new goals of affordable access to the telephone system for schools, libraries and health-care facilities, would, of course, be by open and above board, taxpayer-financed appropriations. While our taxophobic policy-makers are highly unlikely to adopt so straightforward an approach, preferring instead to continue to use such off-budget devices as regulated rate structures, there are better and worse ways to use rate structures for such purposes. As the Commission clearly recognizes and proclaims, to its credit, the worst way is through usage charges, which discourage exactly what we want to encourage. The efficient way would be through fixed charges that explicitly identify the subsidies and what they are paying for. One important advantage of making the cost of subsidizing these various services explicit and visible is that it is likely to cause the public to insist that its total amount be drastically compressed, by making the subsidies available only to customers who truly need the support in order to remain on the network. It makes absolutely no sense to hold telephone rates below costs to all subscribers.

- We depart from that rule for telephone service—underpricing the service to *all* buyers—only because we happen to subject this industry to full-blown economic regulation. The historical rationalization of that kind of regulation, however, has been the perceived need, in the absence of competition, to protect consumers generally from exploitation by what we have generally conceived to be natural monopolies, and the guiding principle of that regulation has therefore been to emulate the results that competition would produce if it were feasible. Those results would *not* include pricing some services far above economic costs and others far below.[177]

- To the extent we continue to finance this service out of a universal service fund, it is essential to bear in mind that no tax levied to provide that fund can ever be wholly "competitively neutral." While it would clearly be an improvement over the present reliance primarily on inflated toll and carrier access charges if the tax applied also to bypass facilities commercially supplied, I am aware of no method that has been proposed that would equivalently tax private carriage—in effect, private bypass.[178]

- Even if "competitively neutral," "equiproportional" taxes, whether on all customer bills or service providers (including self-providers) were feasible, they would still be grossly inefficient, because, in contrast with second-best pricing, they would ignore the relative elasticities of demand for the services whose prices would be inflated by them.

- As I have already suggested, there is evidence that subscription to telephone service is influenced at least as much by the level of

---

[177] See my similar argument in opposition to commissions requiring electric utility companies to subsidize investments in conservation by their customers, except to the extent that rates are below incremental costs and, therefore, inefficiently encourage consumption. "An Economically Rational Approach to Least-Cost Planning for Electric Power," *The Electricity Journal*, Vol. 4, No. 5, June 1991, pp. 11-20.

[178] The tax is to be levied only on carriers that offer telecommunications services directly to the public. *Universal Service Order*, par. 777.

long-distance rates as by the basic monthly charge.[179] There has been no indication at all that such rate rebalancing as various states have engaged in—and the FCC's own rebalancing when it reduced carrier access charges and substituted the $3.50 per month subscriber line charge on all residential bills—resulted in a decline in subscription. Further rebalancing, is therefore, unlikely to conflict with maintenance of the present, almost universal, sub-scribership, particularly if accompanied by targeted subsidies. There is, therefore, no justification whatever for the present, still unbalanced, structure of prices. It is only political timidity—and misguided "consumerism"—that prevents its correction.

In contrast with the courage that it displayed in the 1980s in substituting the fixed subscriber line charge for a large portion of the carrier access charges, the 1997 FCC acted for all the world as though a repetition of that very sensible action would be politically suicidal. In fact, there was a great hue and cry in Congress when the FCC announced its intention to make that change,[180] yet once it went into effect the issue practically disappeared from sight. I had the same experience when, under my chairmanship, the New York Public Service Commission raised basic residential service rates and correspondingly reduced intrastate long-distance charges; it took another such step under my successor. So far as public response is concerned, this rate rebalancing and, I understand, similar ones introduced by such states as California, Illinois, Massachusetts, Michigan and Wisconsin, proved to be virtual non-events—at least there were no reported fatalities among commissioners.[181]

Meanwhile, the *private* response of consumers to the offsettingly reduced long-distance charges was to use their phones far more freely to

---

[179] See note 15, above.

[180] The Commission's original proposal was to go all the way in eliminating the distortion at the interstate level, imposing a subscriber line charge for residences of $7.00 a month rather than the still far from insignificant $3.50 on which it ultimately settled under political pressure.

[181] Duesterberg and Gordon, *op. cit.*, pp. 40-43, 82, 90.

talk to their parents, children and relatives—a palpable improvement in their way of life, collectively.

In view of this history, it is sad to see what the 1997 Commission was saying about the size of the proposed Universal Service Fund and how it was evidently planning to raise it. As for the first, all the brave initial talk on the part of its spokesmen of raising some $15 to $20 billion necessary to replace the gross overcharges for carrier access and long-distance service, the Commission was now talking about $3 to $4 billion a year

> [t]o begin to pay for basic telephone service for poor, disabled, and rural customers, *as well as* for [the new program of] wiring schools, libraries and isolated health care centers,[182]

and

> postpon[ing] the important step of determining how big the actual subsidies ought to be.[183]

If these announcements had signaled an intention to restrict the beneficiaries to "the poor, disabled, rural customers," it would be a cause for rejoicing at the triumph of economic principle and political courage. But that would mean a corresponding increase in the basic service rates to all the non-poor, non-disabled and non-rural customers—and that was obviously the last thing the 1997 FCC intended to do, or that Congress intended it to do.

---

[182] "AT&T Takes Lead on a Plan to Cut Long-distance Cost," *The New York Times*, May 4, 1997, p. 1 f. (stress supplied)

[183] "AT&T Offers to Cut Basic Rates if FCC Trims Access Fees Paid to Local Carriers," *The Wall Street Journal*, May 5, 1997, p. A3 f.

VI. The Political Economy of Disingenuousness—
Concealing Costs and Proclaiming Benefits

The Governor of one of our large states, shortly after taking office, abandoned the strict hands-off policy followed by his predecessors in matters concerning his supposedly independent public utility commission and adopted the practice of having all announcements of rate cuts come out of his office, while leaving announcements of increases to the commission.

The FCC's three major actions of May 7, 1997, in its proceedings involving access reform, universal service and revision of its rate cap formulas, were preceded by a widely publicized announcement of an agreement between AT&T and the Consumer Federation of America involving cuts in the FCC-mandated carrier access charges, on the one side, and a promise by AT&T to reduce its own long-distance rates to all residential customers—in particular the ones that had been neglected until then:

> households that do not subscribe to a discount package for long-distance usage, roughly half of AT&T's seventy-five million customers[184]—

a deal enthusiastically endorsed by Chairman Hundt as

> the key breakthrough in this humongous lobbying battle,

which

> would provide 'the first broadly visible, tangible benefit' of the sweeping telecommunications law enacted last year.[185]

Two days later, the Chairman was even more rhapsodic, characterizing the

---

[184] *The New York Times, op. cit.*, May 4, 1997, p. 1.

[185] *The Wall Street Journal, op. cit.*, May 5, 1997, p. 3 f.

Commission's *Universal Service* and *Access Charge Orders* as responsible for "the single best day for consumers in this agency's history."[186]

A. "Residential Bills Are Going to Go Up"

In view of the many warnings by the CFA in preceding weeks that the only fruit of the new Act was likely to be "higher residential bills" and the Federation's consistent demagogic identification of the "consumer interest" with the basic residential charge, the FCC had obviously decided that jubilant public proclamation of consumer benefits accompanied by concealment of costs to the economy—and consumers at large—was the better part of valor. The fact is, however, that

- the welfare of consumers in the aggregate would have called for an increase in the basic residential charge, accompanied by reductions—either regulatorily imposed or flowing from intensified competition—in charges for carrier access, long-distance, dial-tone to businesses in metropolitan areas and vertical services.

- To the extent bills for the majority of residential customers who make few long distance calls were to go up not just because of the rebalancing of basic and toll rates but also because basic rates to *business* were to go down, only the ignorant—including, evidently, the Consumer Federation of America—would conclude that "consumers" were worse off, evidently on the assumption that consumers escape the burden when businesses are overcharged for telephone services and, correspondingly, do not benefit when charges to businesses are reduced.

- Residential *bills* are likely to go up, additionally, as households respond to the correspondingly reduced long-distance rates by increasing their usage; but such an increase would obviously not be indicative of a loss in welfare. Consumers' "bills" for computers

---

[186] *State Telephone Regulation Report*, May 15, 1997, p. 1.

have undoubtedly skyrocketed in the past 10 years in response to their decreasing price, but no rational person would interpret the consequent increase in outlays as injurious to them.

- The experience of the previous several years provided ample basis for a concern that any offsetting reductions in carrier access charges would not necessarily be reflected in equivalent reductions in long-distance rates across the board. AT&T's basic rates to residential users, the majority of whom did not (at least until 1997) qualify for any of its discount plans, went up 24.7 percent in the five years from the beginning of 1992 to the close of 1996,[187] with MCI and Sprint following in lock step, while access charges went down.[188] AT&T's agreement with the CFA was obviously intended

---

[187] Cumulative increase was calculated from reports in contemporaneous news accounts (table available on request).

[188] We must, of course, consider the possibility that the dramatic difference between this trend and that of long-distance charges to large businesses, which have gone down drastically in the past decade or so, represented a correction of a previous distortion—a cross-subsidization of basic residential by business charges—such as would be expected to take place with the introduction of effective competition. This is the claim of B. Douglas Bernheim and Professor Robert D. Willig ("An Analysis of the MFJ Line of Business Restrictions," Dec. 1, 1994, Attachment G, Ex Parte Presentation in Support of AT&T's Motion for Reclassification as a Nondominant Carrier, CC Docket No. 79-252, Apr. 20, 1995): that the cost per minute of serving low-volume customers is significantly higher than of serving high-volume ones because of the presence of fixed customer costs, such as billing, collections, fraud and customer service, that do not vary with usage for any given subscriber.

For purposes of testing this possible justification of the large increase in AT&T's long-distance charges net of access fees to small residential users, Timothy J. Tardiff and I used the Company's own definition of low-volume residential customers as ones with long-distance charges of $10 per month or less. These are the people who pay the basic rates that had been subject to the 1991-96 increases (Letter of C.L. Ward to W.F. Caton dated March 9, 1995, Re: Ex Parte Presentation CC Dockets Nos. 79-252, 93-197, 80-286; D.J. Quinn, *The Light User Segment of the Long Distance Market*, March 8, 1995, p. 8). AT&T says that more than half of its customers fall in this category. It also asserts that customers with average monthly bills under $3 are below the "break even point." (*Ibid.*) This claim suggests that, to the extent these last customers can be segregated, rates charged them would indeed be expected to increase under real-world competitive conditions, even though presumably the *marginal* costs of their long-distance *calling* would be no higher than

(continued...)

to respond to the legitimate complaint that competition had been far more effective in benefiting big business than small residential customers. But observe how thoroughly *regulatory* is such a response to the demonstrated insufficiency of competition, about which the FCC itself had complained only a short while ago.[189] It

---

(*...continued*)

for higher-volume customers. (That is to say, under theoretically pure competition, under which rates for usage would be held to marginal [usage-sensitive] costs, the higher *average* costs of the very low-volume users would not be reflected in usage rates higher than those charged heavier users. Since, however, the former customers would in those circumstances not be worth serving at all, providers of long-distance service to them would have to be compensated for the fixed per-customer costs either by levying a flat charge on them or by finding a way of charging them discriminatorily higher rates for usage.) But it would neither explain nor justify the increases in basic usage rates undiluted by discount offerings that at least half of residential users had been forced to pay, on grounds of either *average* cost per customer or marginal cost of usage: the group in the $3 to $10 per month range, with four times the usage of the ones below AT&T's claimed $3 break-even point, must have been making a large contribution to company profits even before the 1991-96 rate increases.

[189] Even as it proceeded to grant AT&T non-dominant status, the Commission expressed dissatisfaction with the pattern of price leadership into which the major IXCs had fallen and its consequences for basic residential rates:

> 81. .... since 1991, basic schedule rates for domestic residential service have risen approximately sixteen percent (in nominal terms), with much of the increase occurring since January 1, 1994 ....

> 82. .... each time that AT&T raised its basic rates, MCI and Sprint quickly matched the increase .... [t]his is not evidence of AT&T's individual market power, but perhaps of tacit price coordination.

> 83. We find that the evidence in the record is conflicting and inconclusive as to the issue of tacit price coordination among AT&T, MCI, and Sprint with respect to basic schedule rates or residential rates in general .... To the extent, however, that tacit price coordination may be occurring, the Commission would view this as a matter of serious concern. We believe, however, that this problem, to the extent it may exist, is a problem generic to the interexchange industry and not specific to AT&T. We thus believe these concerns are better addressed by removing regulatory requirements that may facilitate such conduct, such as the longer advance notice period currently applicable only to AT&T, and by addressing the potential issues raised by these concerns in the context of the proceeding we intend to initiate to examine the interstate, domestic, interexchange market as a whole. (*Order, In the Matter of Motion of AT&T to be Reclassified as a Non-Dominant Carrier*, FCC 95-427, Oct. 12, 1995, pars. 81-83; some footnote references omitted.)

is not at all clear how AT&T's pledge could be either enforced or failures to live up to it detected. Its rates would, of course, continue to be unregulated, and the Company could legitimately alter them, both upward and downward, in response to all possible changes in costs and market conditions, including the new fees the FCC imposed on them in its *Access Charge Reform* decision, while simultaneously reducing the access charges themselves (see B., below). In these circumstances, there would be no way of detecting whether the rates it actually charged were lower than they otherwise would have been by the full amount of the reduction in its access charges.[189a]

- The proper cure for the inadequacy of competition for the patronage of small residential customers is to proceed promptly to eliminate the prohibition of the BOCs providing interLATA service, as the Act clearly contemplates. In those instances in which local telephone companies have already been permitted to enter that market, they have done so with substantial rate cuts. This is not surprising considering that (1) they already served all those residential customers, including the ones the volume of whose toll calling alone was too small to qualify them for discounts, and could add long-distance service to their offerings at very low incremental costs, and (2) beginning with a zero market share, they found it necessary in order to make any inroads into the dominating market shares of the incumbent long-distance companies.

[189a] Unsurprisingly, therefore—particularly in view of the FCC-imposed new fees—a dispute soon arose about whether the long-distance companies were living up to the agreement:

> "Long-Distance Providers Accused of Overcharging" – The nation's top three long-distance companies appear to be overcharging telephone customers and blaming the new Federal fees, the chairman of the Federal Communications Commission said today.

> The chairman, Bill Kennard, said the new fees were supposed to be offset by commission-ordered reductions in other fees that long-distance companies pay.

> But it does not appear that the companies have passed along some $1 billion in reductions to their customers, as they had pledged, Mr. Kennard said.

(continued...)

B. The Proposed Sources of the Funds

Joe Louis once said, when asked about his forthcoming championship bout with Billy Conn, "He can run but he can't hide." The Federal Communications Commission seems determined to demonstrate that what Billy Conn was unable to do in the ring, it can readily do in the political and regulatory arena.

Before proceeding to explain why the Commission's "reform" efforts strike me as deserving only a single cheer, it seems only fair to re-emphasize how limited were the options available to it. As I have already pointed out, its jurisdiction comprises only the rates for interstate services and recovery of the costs either causally associated with or allocated to those services, including 25 percent of the costs of loops. This means that its ability to mitigate the extreme inefficiencies in the present structure of rates for telecommunication services is confined, so far as its direct authority is concerned, to the flat subscriber line charge that it imposed in the '80s and the access charges to providers of long-distance services interstate that the SLC partially replaced. Given the hostility in Congress and among highly vocal consumer groups to any direct increase in the first of these charges, it was hardly surprising that, while clearly recognizing what "the right thing" would entail, the Commission betrayed equally its lack of the right stuff to do it.

Unsurprisingly, therefore, its *Access Reform* decision reads as though it were written by a schizophrenic. On the one side, it contains an admirably clear and compelling exposition of the inefficiency of recovering in charges for usage costs that do not vary with usage—preponderantly, the cost of the loop (pars. 36-41). On the other, it almost immediately expresses a determination *not* to increase the subscriber line charge on *primary* lines, justifying that refusal on the undeniable—but also demagogic—tendency of consumer groups and members of Congress to

---

(...*continued*)

AT&T, MCI and Sprint say they have passed along those reductions and disputed Mr. Kennard's suggestions that they may be overcharging customers.

The New York Times, Feb. 27, 1998, p. A12.

identify the "affordability" of the basic service that they have expressed determination to preserve with holding those charges at their present levels.

Where, then, could the Commission hope to recover the reduction in access charges that it had promised[189b] and the costs of the newly subsidized "universal services" to libraries and other such worthy institutions, for which alone it was willing at the time to make explicit, "competitively-neutral" provision? There appeared to be three possibilities, and it embraced all of them:

- an increase in the direct subscriber line charge for second and multiple lines, both residential and business, and

- a flat charge per presubscribed line (so called PIC)—rather than on usage—*to be imposed on and collected by the long-distance carriers.*

- for the universal service fund for schools and the rest, a percentage levy on revenues of both LECs and IXCs (in compliance with the Act) but with the former of these collected by the LECs *via their access charges to the IXCs.*

In a way, one feels compelled to admire the Commission's ingenuity. Like the afore-mentioned Governor, it found a way of proudly announcing a reduction in carrier access charges accompanied by AT&T's promise to pass it on in reduced long distance rates to small residential customers, while leaving it to the long-distance carriers to find ways of passing on to consumers both the PIC and the universal fund obligations

---

[189b] Simultaneously with its *Access Charge Reform* and *Universal Service* decisions, it announced the results of its *Price Cap Performance Review for Local Exchange Carriers* (FCC 97-159), increasing the annual downward productivity adjustment of carrier access charges to 6.5 percent. Manifestly, to the extent it could justify direct reductions in those charges in this way, there was no need to find other means of "financing" them; alternatively put, it could compensate the IXCs in this way for the increases in access charges it employed to collect contributions to the schools and libraries fund, reckoned as a percentage of the revenues of both the LECs and the IXCs.

of the LECs that the Commission decided to impose on them[190]:

- The political case for subsidizing subscription to telephone service applies only to primary lines. It would be difficult for members of Congress or of groups professing to represent the poor to complain about withdrawing those subsidies from all the (putatively) rich people and businesses that subscribe to additional lines.

- Moreover, true to its recognition of the correct economic principles, the Commission proposed to impose those levies in the form of flat charges per line rather than, inefficiently, on usage.

- In neither case, therefore, could it be accused of having behaved inconsistently with the economic principles that it had itself recognized and enunciated.

A churlish economist is obliged to point out, however, that:

- Since the charges on additional lines will be borne preponderantly by businesses, the Commission is in effect catering to the ignorant supposition that such charges are not ultimately borne by "consumers."

- The plausible implicit justification of the increased SLC on second or multiple lines that there is no good social reason for continuing to subsidize them at no point even asks the question

---

[190] Evidently AT&T threatened for a time to pass the buck right back to the Commission, frustrating its obvious attempt to conceal responsibility for the new levy, by showing it as a separate item on its bills; and the FCC bought it off by reducing the charge:

> AT&T said today that for the first half of 1998, it does not plan to assess its residential long-distance customers a separate charge to cover AT&T's contribution to the new universal service fund, including for [sic] schools, libraries and rural healthcare facilities.

> AT&T said this decision regarding residential customers was made in light of the Federal Communications Commission's vote this week to reduce the size of the fund for the first half of 1998. In addition, the company said it will use anticipated reductions in access charges to help offset its contributions to the fund.

AT&T News Release, "AT&T outlines universal service cost recovery plans," for release Dec. 18, 1997.

whether those additional lines are indeed subsidized. The problem, so far as many if not most residential consumers are concerned, is that—as I understand it—the incremental cost of the
second line is *close to zero*, because telephone companies can
and do typically incorporate the necessary wires in their distribution lines when they extend service in the first place, *at a very
low incremental cost,* in order to minimize costs in the long run.
In addition, the demand for second lines must surely be much
more elastic than for first lines. To the extent these are indeed the
facts, the Commission's action is totally inexcusable in the very
economic terms that it has itself enunciated and endorsed.

- Whether or not the incremental costs of extending multiple lines to
  business customers are likewise very low, the flat charges they pay
  for dial tone *are*—at least in urban areas—*generally not subsidized.*
  On the contrary, they tend to be far above incremental costs, in order
  to generate a flow of contribution to basic residential services.[191]

- The Commission has evidently not even considered the possibility that, for these reasons, the surcharge for second and multiple
  lines is economically unjustified in most cases for *both* residences and businesses.

- Finally, there is its decision to transfer a portion of the burden of
  recovering the non-traffic-sensitive costs of subscriber lines and
  of the new subsidizations from usage-based carrier access
  charges to a charge *per* presubscribed *line,* to be collected by the
  IXCs. This will probably be an improvement over the present
  arrangement, on economic efficiency grounds: the demand for
  the *ability* to make toll calls is undoubtedly less elastic than for
  the periodic exercise of that ability, so a flat up-front charge accords with the requirements of second-best efficiency.[192] It would

---

[191] See, e.g., Crandall and Waverman, *op. cit.*, pp. 78, 84.

[192] Actually, so far as the cost of the loop is concerned, if the IXCs do pass the charge
on to their subscribers as a flat rate and that fixed charge cannot be evaded by anyone who subscribes to telephone service (see note 193, immediately following),
the arrangement will turn out to be first-best. That cannot be said of the cost of the
new subsidizations, however.

be foolhardy, however, at the very time when the IXCs, the FCC and Congress are quarreling over the matter, to anticipate in what form those carriers will pass the increased charges on to their subscribers. If their business were perfectly competitive, competition would force them to pass it on in the same form as they incur it—as a flat charge per line. In that event the FCC would have achieved its desired concealment of responsibility for the rate increases by putting the burden on the carriers without sacrifice of economic efficiency.[193] But competition in the long-distance business is surely not perfect, and the IXCs are themselves subject to political constraints. As I have already pointed out (note 188, above), they have, in the recent past, justified the increases in their basic *usage-based* long-distance charges to at least half of their residential customers on the ground that those customers did not make enough long-distance calls for the companies to recover the *fixed costs* of serving and billing them. On the other hand, political considerations might well explain their evident desire to add a new separately identified, flat charge to the bills of their customers, so as not to be accused of rescinding part or all of their previously announced 8 percent reduction in usage charges, as part of the AT&T/CFA bargain.[194] If instead they were simply to compete less

---

[193] If payment of this fee, in effect for the *option* of making long-distance calls, were optional on the part of subscribers—that is, if they could avoid it by refusing to presubscribe to any long-distance carrier—the arrangement would still be inefficient, because providing that option has a zero marginal cost. And while the demand for it is presumably relatively inelastic, the smaller the long-distance usage by any household the larger would the fixed per-line charge bulk in its calculations and the more likely it would be, therefore, simply to give up that option entirely (and inefficiently). The Commission has, however, sagely precluded that escape by authorizing the LECs to impose the flat levy directly on any customers that fail to presubscribe to a long-distance carrier. So, to the extent the IXCs pass the charges on to subscribers in the same flat-rate form as it is imposed on them, the FCC will have succeeded in marrying economic efficiency (of the first-best variety) with either escaping the blame or passing at least some of it on to the long-distance carriers.

[194] On June 30, 1997, evidently in fulfillment of its previous undertaking to the FCC, AT&T announced that it would reduce its basic long-distance rates by 5 percent for day and evening calls and 15 percent for nights and weekends

for the roughly half of AT&T's 75 million customers who are on the basic long-distance plan

(*continued...*)

strenuously henceforward for those customers in what they charge them *per minute of calling*, the FCC would have succeeded even more completely in its attempt at concealment—but only at the cost of violating its laudable expressed intention of reducing or eliminating the inefficiency caused by recovering from usage costs that do not vary with usage.

It ill behooves an economist-believer in the invisible hand, however, to criticize the actions of a regulatory agency on the mere ground that it was motivated by self-interest—even if that self-interest was political rather than economic. The FCC's action imposing the PIC on long-distance carriers, while not as forthright as a direct increase in basic subscriber bills, may well turn out, by the operation of that invisible hand, something like third-best. The fact that those carriers will incur these costs on a per-line basis will give them the incentive to pass it on in the same way, rather than to further discourage usage with charges per minute in excess of marginal costs. Moreover, as Haring and Rohlfs pointed out before the FCC decisions of May 1997,[195] the IXCs will have not merely the incentive but the freedom—recall that their rates are unregulated—to design rates in such a way as to minimize the inefficiency. They could, for example, introduce graduated usage charges, with high initial blocks and end-blocks incorporating volume discounts for demand-elastic traffic—just as it was widely suggested, at the time

---

(...continued)

—reductions that would not be available to customers on discount calling plans. MCI announced that it would follow (*The New York Times*, July 1, 1997, p. D2). As I have already observed, there is or will over time be no way of ascertaining whether or to what extent this reduction reflects the net effect of the FCC's two offsetting actions on the costs of the long distance carriers—the reduction in access charges per minute and the increased flat charge per subscribed line. AT&T's announced intention, understandably, to offset against the reduction in the usage-based access charges the newly-imposed flat PICs, while acceding to the Commission's manifest desire to conceal the latter charge from customers (note 190, above), and the ensuing altercation with the FCC (note 189a), gloriously illustrate Sir Walter Scott's

Oh, what a tangled web we weave,

When first we practice to deceive!

[195] *Op. cit.*, pp. 17-23.

of divestiture, the separated BOCs be permitted to use tapered rate structures to recover their huge non-traffic-sensitive costs thitherto inefficiently allocated to interexchange usage, in order to minimize the
inefficient encouragement of bypass and discouragement of calling.[196]
The apparent failure of this prediction to comport with AT&T's flat reductions in usage charges for small users of long-distance service announced on June 30, 1997, can probably be explained only in terms of
the visible political rather than the invisible economic hand.

---

[196] See, e.g., my "The Road to More Intelligent Telephone Pricing," *Yale Journal on
Regulation*, Vol. 1, No. 2 (1984), pp. 139-157. A precisely analogous arrangement,
embodying a combination of incentives and pricing flexibility, suggests itself as a
method of permitting electric companies to recover whatever portion of their
strandable costs the political process settles upon. The amount of costs that would
otherwise be stranded is unknowable in advance, since it will be the difference between the companies' revenue entitlements, as traditionally determined, and whatever revenues they are able to obtain henceforward in competitive markets. There
is a strong case for setting the amounts of those costs that are to be recoverable on
top of an *estimated* likely course of prices and revenues, in which event the
amounts actually recovered would depend not merely on the course that competitive prices actually take but also, in important degree, on the success or failure of
efforts by the companies themselves to mitigate those strandings—for example, by
promoting sales and improving their efficiency. Promoting sales makes perfectly
good economic sense when marginal costs are far below price, brings closer the
day when excess capacity is exhausted and, by raising the competitive price, automatically reduces the costs that are left stranded. See Miles O. Bidwell and Anna
Della Valle, "Restructuring Rates Creates Value and Reduces Stranded Costs,"
Electricity Journal, Vol. 8, No. 10 (December 1995), pp. 19-25.

VII. The Marasmus of the FCC

Some 45 years ago, Samuel P. Huntington published a thoroughgoing condemnation of the Interstate Commerce Commission, which he entitled "The Marasmus of the ICC."[197] There is no particular point in summarizing his specific criticisms, many of which were, by my standards of 15 to 45 years later, wrong-headed.[198] Translated—at the cost of some distortion of his particular bases for condemning that agency—into the logic that undergirded the economic deregulation movement beginning in the middle 1970s, however, the general argument was unexceptionable: That, whatever the validity of the case for their constitution in the first place, systems of economic regulation and the commissions charged with their effectuation tend to become anti-competitive and excessively protectionist of the interests of the regulated companies—and, I would add, progressively out of touch and inconsistent with evolving economic and technological realities.

That came to be the consensus view of airline (as well as trucking and railroad) regulation during the 1970s, when the major continuing defenders of the pervasive regulatory system were the regulated companies themselves and their labor unions.[199] Shrewdly, therefore, Darius Gaskins—whom I had, to my credit, appointed as chief economist at the Civil Aeronautics

---

[197] "The Marasmus of the ICC: the Commission, the Railroads, and the Public Interest," *Yale Law Journal*, Vol. 61 (April 1952), pp. 467-509. See also Charles S. Morgan, "A Critique of 'The Marasmus of the ICC: the Commission, the Railroads, and the Public Interest," *Yale Law Journal*, Vol. 62, Jan. 1953, pp. 171-225.

[198] The same would be true of many of the criticisms of the Huntington article by Morgan, as well. Essentially both of these extended commentaries accepted the need for continuing thoroughgoing regulation of the transportation industries, with Huntington's major criticisms of the ICC that it was excessively subservient to the interest of the railroads and Morgan's response denying the charge.

[199] "Deregulation and Vested Interests: The Case of Airlines," *The Political Economy of Deregulation*, Roger G. Noll and Bruce M. Owen, eds., American Enterprise Institute Studies in Government Regulation, 1983.

Board—one day proposed that we present to Congress a five-year projected budget, embodying a commitment to regular, sharp percentage reductions toward zero over that period of time—as both an earnest of our deregulatory intentions and as a discipline forcing upon us what might prove to be difficult choices as time unfolded—in much the same way as the rate caps that have become the most general form of rate regulation in telecommunications impose a similar commitment and force hard but socially beneficent choices upon the regulated companies themselves.

The recent history of the FCC is now the latest exemplar of the tendency to "marasmus"—although not exactly the morbid "wasting away" that Huntington's characterization implied. It is necessary, in fairness, to commiserate once again with the Commission on the immensity of the task imposed upon it by the Telecommunications Reform Act and to recognize, one last time, that the ultimate responsibility lies not with it but with a Congress and a public that demand massive investments in a modern telecommunications infrastructure, ubiquitously extended, along with increased competition for residential customers, all with no increases in basic residential rates. The Commission is entitled to give the same kind of answer as Yogi Berra gave when asked why he had missed three consecutive fly balls while substituting in the outfield: "Hank Bauer's screwed up right field so bad, nobody can play it!" The same observation may well apply to Congress and the public.

Nevertheless—if only *because* it has been given an impossible task— the FCC's actions of the past two years strongly suggest that it either is or will soon be ripe for the Gaskins prescription.[200] Its "marasmus" may be the final demonstration we need of the bankruptcy of our current national telecommunications policies.

---

[200] For a set of specific proposals, see Kenneth Gordon and Paul Vasington, *The FCC's Common Carrier Bureau: An Agenda for Reform*, Washington, D.C.: Citizens for a Sound Economy, Sept. 26, 1997. For a radical solution, powerfully advocated, see Peter Huber, *Law and Disorder in Cyberspace, Abolish the FCC and Let Common Law Rule the Telecosm*, Oxford: Oxford University Press, 1997. Also Duesterberg and Gordon, *op. cit.*, Chapter 4 and especially pp. 92-95, "Thinking the Unthinkable."